THE USBORNE

INTERNET-LINKED

COMPLETE BOOK OF

CHESS

COMPLETE BOOK OF

CHESS

THE USBORNE

INTERNET-LINKED

COMPLETE BOOK OF

CHESS

Elizabeth Dalby

Designed by Adam Constantine and Ruth Russell

Consultant: Jonathan Rowson

Chess board illustrations by Verinder Bhachu
and Adam Constantine
Illustrations by Leonard Le Rolland
Digital imagery by Keith Furnival

Cover designer: Neil Francis
Managing designer: Ruth Russell
Managing editor: Judy Tatchell

SCHOLASTIC INC.
New York   Toronto   London   Auckland   Sydney
Mexico City   New Delhi   Hong Kong   Buenos Aires

Contents

Internet linking

Throughout this book, we have suggested interesting Web sites where you can find out more about chess.

Web site links

To visit the sites, go to the Usborne Quicklinks Web site at **www.usborne-quicklinks.com** and type the keywords "complete chess". There you will find links to click on to take you to all the recommended sites. Here are some of the things you can do on the Web sites:

● Discover new chess tactics and tricks
● Read the latest chess news
● Find out all about the history of chess.

Chess puzzles

In Usborne Quicklinks there are also chess puzzles that you can print out to test the skills that you have learned from this book. Just go to **www.usborne-quicklinks.com** and follow the instructions there.

Online chess games

Lots of chess Web sites feature the chance to play chess online against opponents of all abilities. If you want to play chess online, you should ask permission of an adult before you do, and make sure you follow the safety guidelines given at the top of the next column.

Computer not essential

If you don't have access to the Internet, don't worry. This book is a complete, self-contained reference book on its own.

Internet safety

When using the Internet, please make sure you follow these guidelines:

● Ask your parent's or guardian's permission before you connect to the Internet.
● If you write a message in a Web site guest book or on a Web site message board, or take part in an online chess game, do not give out any personal information such as your full name, address or telephone number, and ask an adult before you give your e-mail address.
● If a Web site asks you to log in or register by typing your name or e-mail address, ask permission of an adult first.
● If you do receive an e-mail from someone you don't know, tell an adult and do not reply to the e-mail.
● Never arrange to meet anyone you talk to or play against on the Internet.

Note for parents and guardians

The Web sites described in this book are regularly reviewed and the links in Usborne Quicklinks are updated. However, the content of a Web site may change at any time and Usborne Publishing is not responsible for the content on any Web site other than its own.

We recommend that children are supervised while on the Internet, that they do not use Internet Chat Rooms, and that you use Internet filtering software to block unsuitable material.

Please ensure that your children read and follow the safety guidelines printed above. For more information, see the "Net Help" area on the Usborne Quicklinks Web site.

Using the Internet

Most of the Web sites listed in this book can be accessed with a standard home computer and a Web browser (the software that enables you to display information from the Internet). We recommend:

- A PC with Microsoft® Windows® 98 or later version, or a Macintosh computer with System 9.0 or later, and 64Mb RAM
- A browser such as Microsoft® Internet Explorer 5, or Netscape® 6, or later versions
- Connection to the Internet via a modem (preferably 56Kbps) or a faster digital or cable line
- An account with an Internet Service Provider (ISP)
- A sound card to hear sound files.

Extras

Some Web sites need additional free programs, called plug-ins, to play sounds, or to show videos, animations or 3-D images. If you visit a site and do not have a necessary plug-in, a message will come up on the screen. There is usually a button that you can click on to download the plug-in. Or, go to **www.usborne-quicklinks.com** and click on "Net Help". There you can find links to download plug-ins. Here is a list of plug-ins that you might need:

- RealPlayer® – lets you play video and hear sound files
- QuickTime – enables you to view video clips
- Flash™ – lets you play animations
- Shockwave® – lets you play animations and interactive programs.

Site availability

The links in Usborne Quicklinks are regularly reviewed and updated, but occasionally you may get a message that a site is unavailable. This might be temporary, so try again later, or even the next day. If any of the sites close down, we will, if possible, replace them with suitable alternatives, so you will always find an up-to-date list of sites in Usborne Quicklinks.

Help

For general help and advice on using the Internet, go to Usborne Quicklinks at **www.usborne-quicklinks.com** and click on "Net Help". To find out more about how to use your Web browser, click on "Help" at the top of the browser, and then choose "Contents and Index". You'll find a searchable dictionary containing tips on how to find your way around the Internet easily.

Computer viruses

A computer virus is a program that can seriously damage your computer. A virus can get into your computer when you download programs from the Internet, or in an attachment (an extra file) that arrives with an e-mail. We strongly recommend that you buy anti-virus software to protect your computer and that you update the software regularly. For more information about viruses, go to Usborne Quicklinks and click on "Net Help".

Playing chess

The game of chess has been described as an art, a science and a sport. Almost anyone can learn how to play. Some top chess champions can earn millions – so it could be worth spending time on improving your game.

The mission

The main objective in chess is to trap your opponent's King. Don't forget – all the other moves that you make in the game should build towards this.

Stages of the game

The game has three stages:

The opening
When you try to bring all your pieces into play and develop your plan of attack. (See pages 32–43.)

Forward march!

The middlegame
When you and your opponent battle for control of the board by taking each other's pieces. (See pages 44–49.)

Out of my way!

The endgame
When there are very few pieces left. Your King may become a more active attacking piece as it is in less danger of being attacked. (See pages 62–69.)

Gotcha!

A way of thinking

Wherever you are in a game, you should have a plan that governs how you move your pieces. Stay flexible, though, and change your plan if your opponent does something unexpected.

Don't try to plan too many moves in advance. Even champions don't tend to think ahead very far during a game of chess. There are just too many possibilities.

You can use various tactics, tricks and traps to outwit your opponent.

Setting up the board

The chess board has 64 squares of alternating colours. A "white", or lighter-coloured, square is always positioned at the player's right. The pieces are placed as shown below.

Internet link
For a link to an excellent general chess Web site intended for new chess players go to **www.usborne-quicklinks.com**

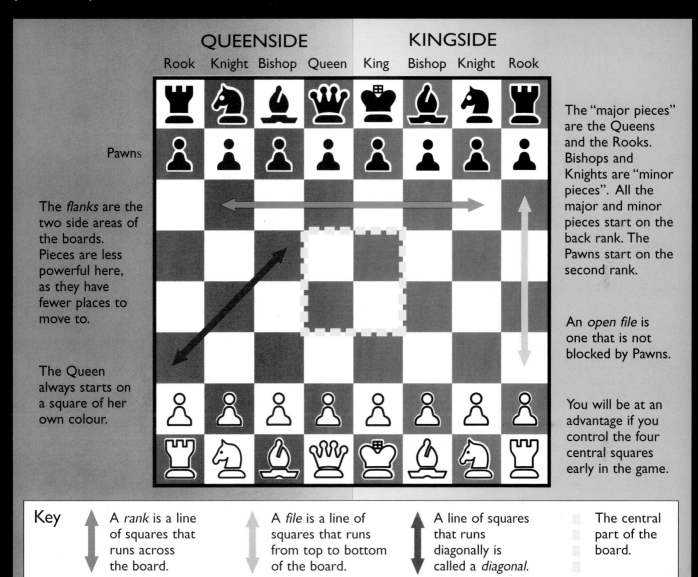

QUEENSIDE   KINGSIDE

Rook   Knight   Bishop   Queen   King   Bishop   Knight   Rook

Pawns

The *flanks* are the two side areas of the boards. Pieces are less powerful here, as they have fewer places to move to.

The Queen always starts on a square of her own colour.

The "major pieces" are the Queens and the Rooks. Bishops and Knights are "minor pieces". All the major and minor pieces start on the back rank. The Pawns start on the second rank.

An *open file* is one that is not blocked by Pawns.

You will be at an advantage if you control the four central squares early in the game.

Key			
A *rank* is a line of squares that runs across the board.	A *file* is a line of squares that runs from top to bottom of the board.	A line of squares that runs diagonally is called a *diagonal*.	The central part of the board.

Key words

diagonal A line of diagonal squares.

file A line of squares from top to bottom.

flank One of the side areas of the board.

Kingside The four files on the King's side.

open file A file that is not blocked by Pawns.

Queenside The four files on the Queen's side.

rank A line of squares from left to right.

Did you know?

Some chess sets are fabulously expensive, made of silver, gold, carved stone or jade. The pieces shown here are from a set made entirely of glass. The "white" pieces are clear and the "black" pieces are frosted.

Writing chess down

The standard way to record chess moves and games of chess is called *algebraic notation*. You will see this kind of notation in chess books, newspapers or on Web sites. Each square on the board has a different code, and so does each chess piece.

How the squares are coded

Each file is given a letter and each rank has a number. This means that each square has its own code. The letter comes first when you write down the code of a square. For example, the white King is on square **e1**.

In diagrams, White always starts on the first two ranks, at the bottom of the board. Black always starts on ranks seven and eight, at the top of the board.

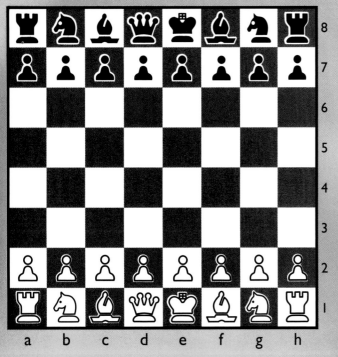

The board diagrams in this book are numbered and lettered to help you work out the code for each square.

How the pieces are coded

All the pieces except the Pawns have codes:

King = K		Knight = N	
Queen = Q		Bishop = B	
Rook = R		Pawn = no code	

Other letters can be added after the move code to describe the move further:

+	Check	(Q)	Pawn promotes to Queen	
++	Checkmate	(N)	Pawn promotes to Knight	
0-0	Kingside castle	x	A capture (this is written immediately after the piece code)	
0-0-0	Queenside castle			
!	Good move			
=	Neither side has the advantage			

All these terms are explained later on.

Writing moves down

Number each pair of moves – write White's move first. Write the code letter of the piece, then the letter and number of the square it is moving to. (For a Pawn, just write down the square it is moving to.) For example:

1. d4 d5   **2. e4 c6**   **3. e5 Bf5**

(Black's moves are written as **1... d5**. The dots after the number show that White's move is missing.)

Did you know?

The number of possible different games of chess is greater than the number of atoms in the known universe.

How the diagrams work

The games and puzzles in this book are described using diagrams as well as algebraic notation. Here is what the different symbols on the diagrams mean:

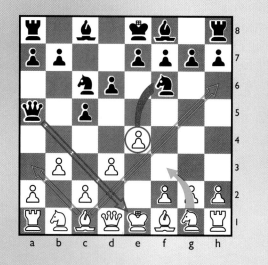

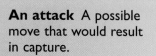

A move The new position of a piece after one turn.

A capture A piece taken when an enemy lands on its square.

An attack A possible move that would result in capture.

A possible move A square that a piece could be moved to.

Key words

algebraic notation The standard method of writing down chess games, using letters and numbers to identify squares on the board, and letter codes for the pieces.

Internet link
For a link to a Web site where you can browse a selection of beginners' chess games, illustrated with diagrams and algebraic notation, go to **www.usborne-quicklinks.com**

How chess pieces move

The six types of chess piece have different moves:

 King

Can move one square in any direction. Cannot move to a square that is under attack from an opposing piece or jump over pieces.

 Queen

Can move any number of squares in a straight line along any open rank, file or diagonal. Cannot jump over pieces.

 Rook

Can move any number of squares in a straight line along any open rank or file. Cannot jump over pieces.

 Bishop

Can move any number of squares in a straight line along open diagonals. Always stays on squares of the same colour. Cannot jump over pieces.

 Knight

Can move in an "L" shape in any direction – two squares forward and one square to the left or right. Can jump over other pieces.

 Pawn

Can move one square forward, except first move, when it may move forward two squares. Can capture on either of two squares diagonally ahead.

The King

The two Kings are the most important pieces on the board. If either is captured, the game is over. However, they are not the most powerful pieces. You should use your other pieces to protect the King from attack.

Piece value
Invaluable (if the King is captured, the game is over)

Special moves
Castling (with Rook)

The shape of this King chess piece symbolizes the crown that a king wears to show his power.

If the King cannot escape capture, its importance counts for nothing – the game is over.

The King's move in detail

The King can go in any direction, one square at a time. It therefore cannot move fast enough to be an attacking piece in the early stages of the game. In the endgame, when there are fewer pieces left on the board, you can use the King as part of your attack.

The King has more possible moves when it is near the middle of the board. However, it is also exposed to attack from all sides.

Be careful when your King is trapped near the edges or corners of the board. If it can't escape from attack you will lose the game.

King attack!

A King that could be taken by an enemy piece's next move is said to be in *check*.

Check!

If your King is in check, you must do one of the following to stop the check:

● Capture the *checking piece*.
● Move your King out of check.
● Position another piece between the attacking piece and your King.

You may never move the King into check.

If it is impossible for the King to escape check, then the game is over. This is called *checkmate*.

The King's role

A King has been part of the game of chess since it began in Asia. The piece was first called the *Rajah*, and later became the *Shah*.

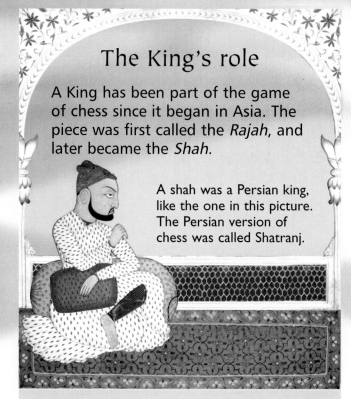

A shah was a Persian king, like the one in this picture. The Persian version of chess was called Shatranj.

When the modern game of chess evolved in Europe around the fifteenth century, this piece became known as the King. At the same time, it gained an extra move – castling (see right).

This picture of a medieval king shares some of the characteristics of the King in chess. His crown shows his importance. But he is still vulnerable and needs his people to protect him.

Key words

castling A special move for a King and Rook. They change places to protect the King and to bring the Rook into the middle to attack.

check An attack on the King.

checkmate When the King cannot escape from the attack (the game ends).

checking piece A piece that attacks the King.

Defending the King

Castling is a double move for the King and a Rook. It has several advantages. The King moves away from the exposed central files, to a square behind a wall of Pawns that can defend it. This move also brings the Rook to the middle, where it is most effective.

Stick with us.

Each player may only castle once, and only before the King and the Rook have been moved. You may not castle if your King is in check, or if any of the spaces between the King and the Rook are under attack.

Castling Kingside

When the two spaces between the King and the Kingside Rook are clear, the King moves two spaces towards the Rook. The Rook jumps to the space on the other side of the King.

Castling Queenside

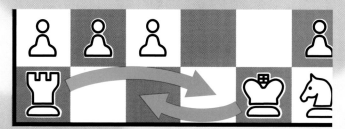

When the three spaces between the King and the Queenside Rook are clear, the King moves two spaces towards the Rook. The Rook jumps to the space on the other side of the King.

Internet link
For a link to a Web site with information and detailed diagrams explaining more about using the castling move, go to
www.usborne-quicklinks.com

Kings on the attack

During the endgame, when most pieces have been taken, the two Kings take on a more attacking role. They may advance towards each other but can never occupy next-door squares. (This is because the two Kings would place each other in check.)

Grrr...

When there is only one square left between two advancing Kings, the player that moved last is said to have the *opposition*. This is an advantage – the other King cannot come any nearer and must move in a different direction. It is possible to gain the opposition by *losing a tempo* (making an extra move to lose time), and this might happen in the following way:

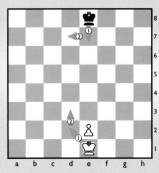

1. Kd2 Ke7
2. Kd3 Kd7
The two Kings advance. White's King has to go around the Pawn.

3. Kd4 Kd6
There is one square left between the Kings. Black has the opposition – White can advance no further.

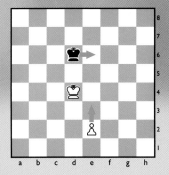

4. e3! Ke6
White moves a Pawn, loses a tempo and regains the opposition. It can now control Black's play.

5. Ke4! Kd6
6. Kf5
White forces Black's King to give way, and should now aim to promote its Pawn.

Trapped King

If you have castled your King, it may seem safe behind a wall of Pawns. However, the Pawns that defend it can also trap it, resulting in *back rank mate* (see below).

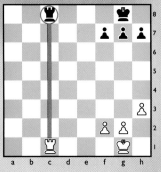

1. Rxc8++
White's Rook takes the black Rook, and checkmates Black at the same time. The black King is trapped on the back rank behind its own Pawns.

A good way to guard against this happening is to provide an escape route by moving the h-Pawn one square forward (or the b-Pawn if you have castled Queenside), as shown above by the white pieces.

No escape!

Although you should try to protect your King on all sides, remember that your own pieces could block your King's escape if you are not careful. If this happens it is known as *smothered mate*.

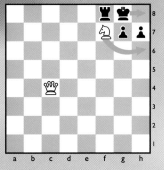

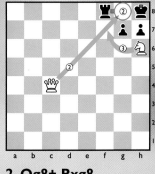

1. Nh6+ Kh8
Black has no choice but to move the King out of check.

2. Qg8+ Rxg8
3. Nf7++
The King is surrounded and can't escape mate.

> ### Did you know?
> The word "checkmate" comes from the Persian expression *shah mat* which means, literally, "the King is dead".

? King puzzles

Can you solve these brainteasing puzzles involving the King?

1. How can White win a piece here?

2. How can White checkmate in one?

3. Can you spot Black's brilliant move to give checkmate?

4. Can you find a two-move checkmating sequence for White?

For puzzle solutions, see page 90.

 Do

- Castle early to protect your King.

- Use your army of pieces to help defend your King.

- Use your King as an attacking piece in the endgame.

Don't

- Block your King's escape routes with your own pieces.

- Leave your King exposed or undefended.

- Try to use your King as an attacking piece too early in the game.

King defence tips

Try to defend open files or diagonals that lead to the King, or it may be vulnerable to attack.

Try not to let your opponent place pieces close to your King.

You may be able to divert an attack on your King by attacking your opponent's King or other important pieces such as the Queen.

Give your King an escape route to avoid either back rank mate or smothered mate.

Try to see your King through the eyes of your opponent – as a moving target.

I'm coming to get you...

Key words

back rank mate The King is trapped on the back rank by other pieces, resulting in checkmate.

losing a tempo In the example shown on the opposite page, White loses a tempo by moving a Pawn instead of the King in order to gain the opposition. It actually means losing time – usually a bad thing, especially in the opening stage of the game, when the race is on to develop your pieces.

opposition When a square separates two advancing Kings, the player that moved last has the opposition.

smothered mate The King is completely surrounded by its own pieces and cannot move out of checkmate.

Internet link
For a link to a Web site that contains an exellent (but advanced) chess tactics glossary, including "gaining the opposition", go to **www.usborne-quicklinks.com**

The Queen

The Queen is the most powerful piece in your army. It is a devastatingly effective attacking piece, sometimes even able to threaten several pieces at once as it can move any distance in any direction. You should therefore use it wisely and avoid losing it at all costs.

The Queen's move in detail

The Queen can move in any direction, along ranks, files and diagonals. It is extremely powerful because it can move any number of squares, as long as its path is not blocked by another piece – its own pieces or the enemy's.

Sorry ma'am you can't pass!

Piece value
Nine (the most valuable piece on the board)

Special moves
None

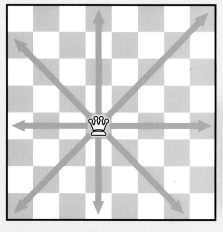

The powerful Queen can move in all directions, for any distance, but it cannot jump over pieces.

The lady is a Queen

The English name for the most powerful chess piece is the Queen, because it stands beside the King. However, in French it is simply called *la dame* (lady), as it is in German (*die Dame*) and Italian (*la donna*).

When the Queen piece was first introduced in 1475, the new version of chess was called the "mad Queen game", as many chess players didn't like the new Queen piece.

It is best not to bring the Queen into play too early, when the board is crowded with pieces and it may be forced to retreat. This would waste time that could be spent using other pieces to mount attacks, such as the Knights or the Bishops.

The Queen usually wears a coronet, and is the second-tallest piece on the board, after the King.

Certain capture

The Queen is a good piece with which to *fork* (threaten two or more pieces belonging to your opponent). Your opponent can only defend one piece at a time, so you will be able to capture the other with your next move. (For more about forks, see page 50.)

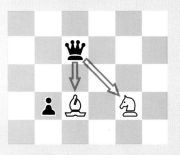

The black Queen forks the white Knight and Bishop. Whatever White does next, it will lose a piece.

 Do

- Use your Queen's attacking power during the middlegame.

- Consider forcing an *exchange* of Queens if you urgently need to take pressure off your King.

 Don't

- Bring your Queen into play too early. If you have to retreat, you may waste valuable time that could be spent developing other pieces.

- Let your Queen be taken without a very good reason, for example to divert attention away from your King if it is under attack.

Key words

fork A sneaky move – a piece moves to a square from where it can threaten two or more opposing pieces at once.

exchange Initiating the loss of one piece to enable you to capture a piece of the same type or value.

A Queen for a Queen

You should try not to allow your Queen to be taken – as far into the game as possible. However, you may decide to force the loss of both Queens (called an *exchange*). For example, if your King is under attack, a Queen exchange may divert your opponent's attention.

Once both Queens are out of the way, the King is safer and can move around the board more. The exchange itself may also divert your opponent from the course of the attack. Below is an example:

1... Qe5+
The black King may be attacked by White's Rook. Black creates a diversion and puts White in check.

2. Qxe5
The white Queen defends the white King by taking Black's threatening Queen...

2... dxe5
...but is immediately taken by a black Pawn. Black has effectively forced a Queen exchange.

3. Rh7+ Kg6
White now attacks Black's King with its Rook, but Black can simply move away unscathed.

Internet link
For a link to an interactive Web site where you can try to place eight Queens on a chess board in such a way that none of them threaten each other, go to **www.usborne-quicklinks.com**

17

The Rooks

Each player has two Rooks. They are extremely powerful – the only piece more powerful is the Queen. Rooks are especially deadly when they work as a team, and they can devastate your opponent's defence to bring checkmate if you use them well.

Piece value
Five

Special moves
Castling*
(with the King)

The name "Rook" came from the Persian word *ruhk*, meaning "chariot". The modern piece may be intended to resemble an ancient battering ram or moveable tower.

The Rook's move in detail

Rooks can move back and forth any number of squares, along ranks and files.

They are very powerful when placed on open files (those that are clear of Pawns and other pieces). Here, a Rook can threaten its opponent from a position deep within its own territory.

Rooks are powerful anywhere on the board, as long as they have open ranks or files to move along.

Pawn protectors

Rooks make good escorts for Pawns that are heading for promotion in the endgame (see page 25). They can give support from behind without blocking the Pawns' progress across the board.

A Rook on the same file as a Pawn protects it from behind.

*For more about castling, see page 13.

Doubly effective

I'm right behind you...

Place your Rooks next to each other on ranks or files, where they can work as a pair to mow down your opponent's pieces. Rooks positioned in this way are called *doubled Rooks*.

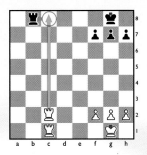

1. Rc8+ Rxc8

The first of White's doubled Rooks tears into enemy lines, giving check to the black King. Black is forced to retaliate by taking the Rook.

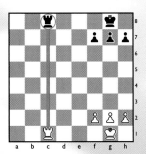

2. Rxc8++

White fires a follow-up shot with the second Rook, taking the black Rook. Black's King has no escape now – it is checkmated.

A well-positioned Rook

The Rooks' effectiveness depends on their position in relation to other pieces. Try to move Rooks to positions where they dominate open files, to control as many squares as possible.

I'm coming through...

1. Re1

The two sides have similar positions, but White moves first – its Rook to an open file. Black cannot now move its own Rook to that file without being taken by White.

Do

- Move Rooks to open files when you can.

- Use Rooks to give support to your Pawns from behind.

- Try to let your Rooks work together. Doubled Rooks are lethal weapons.

- Remember that your Rooks are the most powerful of your pieces after the Queen. Try to keep them until the endgame, when they will prove useful.

Don't

- Let your Rooks become trapped on blocked ranks or files.

- Hamper a Pawn's chances of promotion* by positioning your Rook in front of a Pawn that is trying to reach the other end of the board.

- Sacrifice Rooks carelessly – they are valuable.

Internet link
For a link to a Web site where you can find out the names of the chess pieces in over fifty different languages, go to
www.usborne-quicklinks.com

Key words

doubled Rooks Two Rooks of the same colour on the same rank or file (usually file). Together, they form an extremely powerful attacking force. If one of the Rooks launches an attack, but is taken, the other can immediately attack again from the same place.

*For more about Pawn promotion, see page 25.

The Bishops

The two Bishops are a powerful attacking force, especially when they work together to dominate the board. You should develop your Bishops quickly, but also try to keep both of them as long as you can.

These Bishops are from a chess set of the style, known as Staunton, that is used in tournaments.

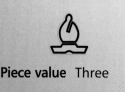

Piece value Three

Special moves None

The top of the Bishop chess piece resembles the hat that a real bishop wears, called a *mitre*.

The Bishop's move in detail

A Bishop can move any number of squares, along diagonals only. It cannot jump over other pieces.

Each player has two Bishops; one starts on a black square and one starts on a white square. As they only move diagonally, each Bishop always stays on squares the same colour as it started on.

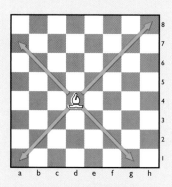

The Bishop can move as far as it likes along the diagonals but it cannot jump over pieces.

Working together

Mm... excellent plan!

The Bishops can be powerful because they have a long range. A pair of Bishops near the centre of the board can control many squares.

When Bishops work together, they can control both the white and the black diagonals so there is no place for your opponent to hide! Remember that if your opponent only has one Bishop (for example, the black-squared Bishop), your pieces will be safer on squares of the other colour (in this case, the white squares).

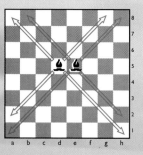

The two Bishops should work together to dominate the board. The diagram shows how many squares they can threaten.

Ready for attack

A sequence of two moves allows the Bishop to control the longest diagonal on the board. This is called *fianchetto*, and leaves the Bishop ready to attack while being protected on three sides by Pawns.

I'm in control here...

1. g3 e5
2. Bg2
The Bishop moves to the Pawn's starting square – *fianchetto*.

The word *fianchetto* comes from an Italian word meaning "side" or "flank" (because the Bishop moves to the side of the board).

> **Internet link**
> For a link to a Web site with a "user's guide to the *fianchetto*", that covers many different aspects of this type of opening move, go to **www.usborne-quicklinks.com**

Good Bishop, bad Bishop

A Bishop that is free to move is called a *good Bishop*. But the Bishop's diagonal move means there is a danger it may tangle with its own Pawns. If it becomes trapped behind them on *closed diagonals*, it is called a *bad Bishop*.

The black Pawns are not obstructing the movement of the black Bishop on this board. This is a good Bishop.

The white Bishop is trapped by its own Pawns. It cannot move freely or very far, so it is called a bad Bishop.

Do

● Develop your Bishops early in the game – possibly using an opening that involves them, like the King's Indian Defence (see page 43).

● Use your Bishops together – they are much more effective when attacking as a pair.

● Try to have good Bishops – don't block their progress with your own pieces.

● Try not to give up a Bishop unless you exchange it for the opposing Bishop on the same colour squares, or you will be more vulnerable to attack.

Don't

● Sacrifice your Bishops if you can avoid it. They are a useful checkmating force in the endgame (for more on the endgame, see pages 62–69).

● Allow bad Bishops (Bishops blocked in by your own Pawns).

● Let your opponent take advantage of undefended diagonals if you only have one Bishop.

Key words

bad Bishop A Bishop that is trapped behind its own Pawns and cannot take part in attacks effectively.

closed diagonal A diagonal blocked by pieces.

fianchetto An opening move that places a Bishop on the longest diagonal.

good Bishop A Bishop that is not trapped by its own pieces and can move freely.

The Knights

E ach player has two Knights. The Knights are good at squeezing into tight spaces on the board, where you can use their jumping power to launch surprise ambushes.

A Knight chess piece usually resembles the head of a horse.

Piece value Three

Special moves
None – but they are able to jump over other pieces as part of their move.

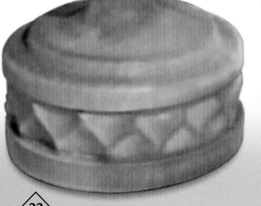

A Knight's jumping move is like a horse leaping over obstacles in its way.

The Knight's move in detail

The Knights move in an "L" shape – two squares in any direction followed by one square to either right or left.

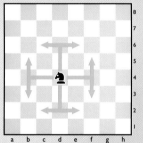

Knights can move in any direction, and may jump over other pieces.

Knights can move before any Pawns do, which can be a useful move during the opening.

Central role

Knights are less powerful near the edges of the board than in the middle. As you can see, the Knight in the middle can move to eight squares, while the one at the edge can move to only four.

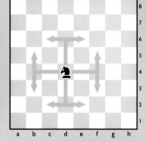

A Knight near the middle of the board can move in any direction.

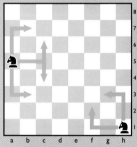

A Knight's movement is limited when it is at the edge of the board.

Strengths and weaknesses

A Knight's move makes it useful when the board is crowded with pieces. The agile Knights can hop between empty squares and weaken the enemy defence or force a smothered mate*.

When there are few pieces left, the Knights may move too slowly to make effective attacks, compared to Rooks or Bishops.

*For more about smothered mate, see page 14.

Do

● Use your Knights to mount surprise attacks on your opponent – they are good at squeezing into gaps between pieces, especially in situations where the board is very crowded with both players' pieces.

● Support your Knights with Pawns. Otherwise, they can be vulnerable to attacks from longer-range pieces. This kind of Pawn support for more valuable pieces is called *anchorage*.

● Place your Knights in *outposts* – these are squares where they can't be attacked by opposing Pawns.

 ## Don't

● Confine your Knights to the edges of the board. The number of squares they can move to is limited. They are even more restricted in the corners where they only have two possible squares that they can move to.

(?) Knight puzzle

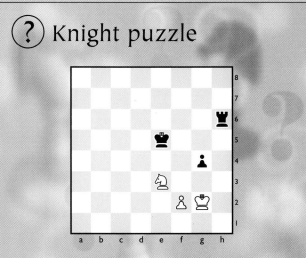

Can you spot a powerful move that White can make to capture a black piece, and then another?

For the puzzle solution, see page 90.

Key words

anchorage Support provided by Pawns for pieces that may be unable to escape from attack quickly, like Knights.

outpost A square that cannot be attacked by opposing Pawns.

Cover me!

Internet link
For a link to a Web site about the Knight's Tour – a famous mathematical problem based on the Knight's move in chess – with information and solutions, go to **www.usborne-quicklinks.com**

Knight wear

In some chess sets, the Knight piece is designed to look like a soldier on horseback. In medieval times, a knight was a mounted soldier who served and protected the King.

This ivory Knight piece is from a 12th-century set. It was found on the Isle of Lewis, in Scotland, and shows a knight on horseback.

The Pawns

Each player has eight Pawns. On their own, they are not very valuable but they can work as a team to attack and defend. If one of your Pawns reaches your opponent's end of the board it can be replaced by a more valuable piece, usually a Queen.

Piece value One

Special moves
- May move one or two squares on first move.
- Diagonal capture.
- The *en passant* rule.

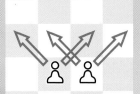

Eight red Pawns line up at the start of a game. Red pieces are often used instead of black in chess sets.

The Pawn's move in detail

A Pawn can only ever move forwards. Usually you can move it only one square; but on its first move you can move it two squares if you prefer.

This slow movement, in one direction only, restricts Pawns. However, if you use them carefully they can work together and support each other as well as providing cover for your other pieces.

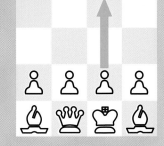

The basic Pawn move – one square forwards along its file.

On its first move, a Pawn can move either one or two squares forwards.

Devious capturing

The Pawns only deviate from their steady forwards march to capture enemy pieces. They make captures by darting diagonally forwards to either left or right.

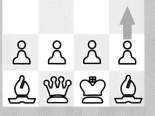

The white Pawn moves one square diagonally forwards to capture an enemy piece, in this case, a black Pawn.

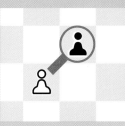

This diagram shows how two Pawns can dominate the important central part of the board by threatening four spaces.

No sneaking past!

There is one rule that allows a Pawn to make a special move, called *en passant*. On its first turn, a Pawn may move two squares forwards. In doing this, it may be possible for the Pawn to sneak past an opposing Pawn. The *en passant* rule allows the Pawn that has been outsmarted to take the sneaky Pawn anyway.

Oi, you – come back here!

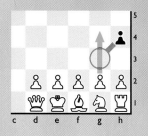

1. g4 xg3
White moves a Pawn forwards two spaces, next to Black's Pawn. If White had moved the Pawn only one square, Black would have been able to capture it.

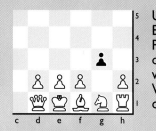

Using the *en passant* rule, Black has taken the white Pawn anyway. It ends up on the square where it would have landed if White had moved only one square ahead.

Pawn promotion

If one of your Pawns manages to reach the other end of the board (its *queening square*), it is *promoted*. This means that you may replace it with a more powerful piece, usually a Queen (because a Queen is the most powerful piece and therefore the most useful).

If your Queen has already been taken, you can have it back to replace the promoted Pawn. If you still have your Queen, you need to make the promoted Pawn look different. You could balance it on top of a Rook that has already been taken, put a ring over it, or even replace it with another small object.

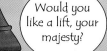

Would you like a lift, your majesty?

Internet link
For a link to a Web site that contains frequently asked questions about the Pawn's moves in chess, go to
www.usborne-quicklinks.com

Key words

en passant The rule that allows a Pawn to capture another that has tried to evade capture by moving forward two squares.

promotion When a Pawn reaches the other end of the board and can be swapped for a more powerful piece, usually a Queen.

queening square The square that a Pawn must reach to gain promotion.

Do

● Use your Pawns to dominate the middle of the board during the opening stage of the game if you can.

● Activate your Pawns in the middlegame – use them to attack enemy pieces and defend your own.

● Give up your Pawns if necessary, to help your other pieces advance.

● Conserve some of your Pawns until the endgame, when they will become powerful if they can promote.

Don't

● Give up your Pawns unneccessarily. They may be worth more than you think – if not now, then later!

● Move the Pawns on the flanks during the opening if you can avoid it – concentrate on the central Pawns.

Strong Pawn positions

Each Pawn marches forwards relentlessly throughout the game. As they cannot go backwards, you need to think very carefully before you move any of your Pawns.

A strong *Pawn structure* can affect your entire strategy, allowing your pieces to work well together in the middlegame. It also means that you will find promoting Pawns easier in the endgame.

Everybody with me? Good.

 Do

● Use your Pawns to support each other. The white Pawns on a2, b3 and c4 form a *Pawn chain*. Black can only safely attack the base of the chain on a2 without risking capture.

White's Pawns support each other, form a strong defence, and don't prevent the other pieces from launching attacks.

● Try to have *passed Pawns* like the white Pawn on e5. This Pawn has no more enemy Pawns to pass on its own or next-door files. It is therefore more likely to reach the other end of the board and gain promotion.

● Use a Pawn on the seventh rank, like the one on g7, to threaten your opponent. This Pawn can safely promote with its next move – Black will be unable to take it immediately.

● Use Pawns to support more valuable pieces like Knights. The Pawn on h4 is supporting the Knight on g5. This method of support is called anchorage*.

● Dominate the middle of the board with Pawns during the opening, use them to attack and defend in the middlegame, and promote them in the endgame.

Did you know?

An unflattering word for an opponent who is a weaker chess player than yourself is a *patzer*. It comes from the German verb *patzen*, which means "to mess up".

Internet links
Go to **www.usborne-quicklinks.com** for links to the following Web sites:

Web site 1 A selection of fascinating chess records, including the most Pawn promotions in a game.

Web site 2 A biography page about Akiba Rubinstein, a chess player famous for his mastery of Pawn structures.

* For more about anchorage, see page 23.

Weak Pawn positions

Problems tend to arise when your Pawn structure gets broken up, or when a tightly-knit Pawn structure gets in the way of your other attacking pieces.

We're losing it, chaps.

The placing of your Pawns directly affects your ability to attack or defend effectively. On the board below are some examples of Pawn structures to try to avoid.

 Don't

• Have *isolated Pawns*, like the one on h6, if you can help it. They make easy pickings for your opponent, especially if not supported by pieces.

• Scatter Pawns in small groups across the board in *Pawn islands,* as both players have done here. Your enemy will have little trouble capturing them. Black's Pawns especially are broken up and not supporting each other.

• Let your Pawns get left behind by the others, like the *backward Pawn* on a2. This Pawn cannot rely on the support of other Pawns in case of attack.

Both players have badly-placed Pawns on this board – they either block each other and other pieces or are separated from the others and so undefended.

• Structure your Pawns in such a way that they impede the movements of your other pieces, like the black-squared Bishop on f8, which can only move to the g7 square. A restricted Bishop is a bad Bishop*.

• Have *double* or *triple Pawns*, like White's double Pawns on the b-file. They cannot support each other.

Key words

backward Pawn A Pawn that has been left behind by the Pawns next to it, and so is undefended.

double Pawns Two Pawns of the same colour on the same file.

isolated Pawn A lone Pawn that is undefended.

passed Pawn A Pawn that has left the opposing Pawns on next-door files behind.

Pawn chain Pawns arranged on next-door squares along a diagonal.

Pawn island A group of Pawns cut off from the others that are therefore vulnerable to attack.

Pawn structure Pawn arrangements on the board.

triple Pawns Three Pawns on the same file.

* For more about bad Bishops, see page 21.

Values, sacrifices and exchanges

Each chess piece has a value. For example, the Queen is given a value of nine, while each Pawn is given a value of one. These values are not used for anything in the game, but they help you to remember how important a piece is.

Piece values at a glance

 King Invaluable. When it is captured, the game is over.

 Queen Nine. The most valuable piece because it is also the most powerful.

 Rook Five. This piece is also very valuable because of its attacking power.

 Bishop Three. Similar in value to the Knights.

 Knight Three. Similar in value to the Bishops.

 Pawn One. Much more valuable if it can be promoted.

Internet link
For a link to a Web site that explains a chess variant for four people that reuses pieces that have been taken, go to **www.usborne-quicklinks.com**

A fair exchange?

The piece values help you to work out whether an *exchange* of pieces with your opponent is fair. (An exchange is a series of moves in which each of you loses a piece.) For example:

Bishop = three   **Knight** = three

Black exchanges a Bishop for a Knight. Pieces of equal value give a *fair exchange*.

Bishop = three   **Rook** = five

Black exchanges a Bishop for a more valuable Rook. Black has made an *advantageous exchange*.

Rook = five   **Knight** = three

Black exchanges a Rook for a Knight. The Rook is more valuable, so Black has made a *sacrifice*.

Key words

advantageous exchange Exchanging a low-value piece for one of higher value.

fair exchange Exchanging similar value pieces.

sacrifice Loss of a piece as part of a strategy.

material gain Having pieces of a higher total value than your opponent after a move or a series of moves.

Exceptions to the value rules

Although the piece values remain fixed, the real importance of a particular piece depends on the stage of the game and also where the piece is on the board at the time.

For example, a Pawn that is on the seventh rank can be promoted with its next move. This means that the Pawn is far more valuable than it would be if it were near the middle of the board.

Also, although a Bishop and a Knight both have a value of three, they may be more or less valuable to you. A Bishop is useful on a board with lots of open diagonals. A Knight is more useful on a board that is cluttered with pieces.

 Do

● Use exchanges and sacrifices as part of your game plan.

● Try to outwit your opponent by making advantageous exchanges.

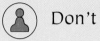 Don't

● Rely too much on the values of the pieces when you are trying to work out whether a sacrifice is a good idea – they are only intended as a guide.

● Forget that some pieces become more valuable later in the game – such as Pawns.

The decision to sacrifice

You may make a sacrifice for immediate *material gain* (to have more valuable pieces than your opponent), or to improve the position of your pieces on the board or to weaken your enemy's defence.

In this sequence, by sacrificing a Rook, White takes the pressure off its King and forces checkmate:

1. Rh8+! Kxh8
The white Rook places the black King in check. Black is forced to take the Rook.

2. Qh5+ Kg8
The white Queen now checks the King, forcing it to retreat.

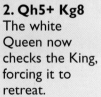

3. Qh7++
One more advance from the Queen and Black is checkmated.

An eight year old girl studies the chess board in a tournament game. Many world champions take up chess at a young age.

Piece puzzles

On these two pages are some puzzles designed to test your knowledge of how the different chess pieces work best in game situations. When you are trying to solve the puzzles, consider the characteristics of each piece, and the way they move.

♘ Knight puzzle

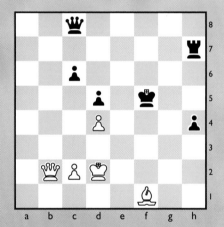

White can make an advantageous exchange by moving its Knight – how?

CLUE:
Look at the squares that the other white pieces are guarding.

♙ Pawn puzzles

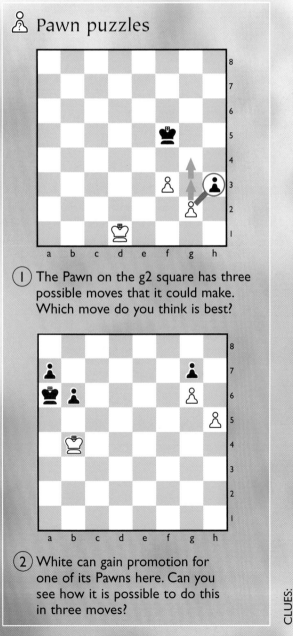

① The Pawn on the g2 square has three possible moves that it could make. Which move do you think is best?

② White can gain promotion for one of its Pawns here. Can you see how it is possible to do this in three moves?

CLUES:
1. Which black piece looks threatening?
2. You should consider sacrificing one Pawn in order to promote another.

♗ Bishop puzzles

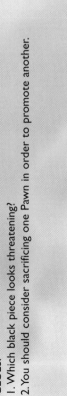

① Find two attacking moves for the white Bishop that will allow it to make a capture on its next move.

② White can use the pair of Bishops to force Black into a checkmate position. Can you see how to do this with one move?

CLUES:
1. A King cannot stay in check.
2. Remember that a King is an attacking piece too.

For puzzle solutions see page 90.

♖ Rook puzzle

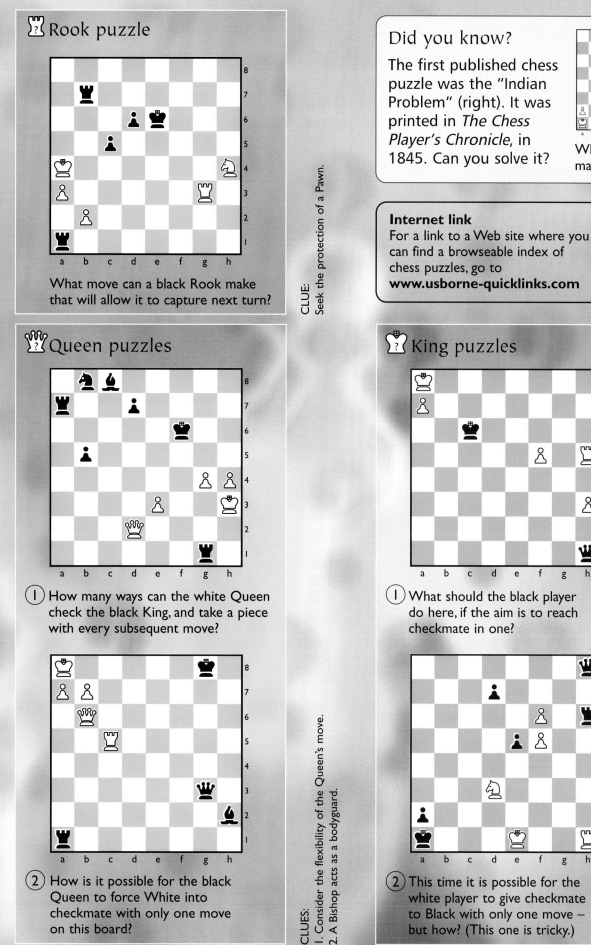

What move can a black Rook make that will allow it to capture next turn?

CLUE:
Seek the protection of a Pawn.

Did you know?

The first published chess puzzle was the "Indian Problem" (right). It was printed in *The Chess Player's Chronicle*, in 1845. Can you solve it?

White to move; mate in four.

Internet link
For a link to a Web site where you can find a browseable index of chess puzzles, go to
www.usborne-quicklinks.com

♕ Queen puzzles

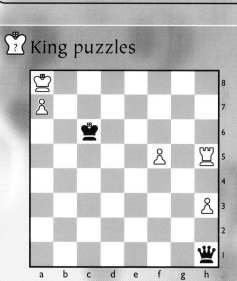

① How many ways can the white Queen check the black King, and take a piece with every subsequent move?

② How is it possible for the black Queen to force White into checkmate with only one move on this board?

CLUES:
1. Consider the flexibility of the Queen's move.
2. A Bishop acts as a bodyguard.

♔ King puzzles

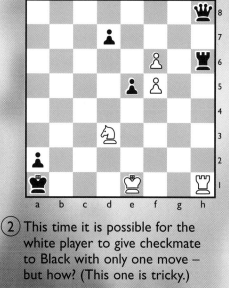

① What should the black player do here, if the aim is to reach checkmate in one?

② This time it is possible for the white player to give checkmate to Black with only one move — but how? (This one is tricky.)

CLUES:
1. Think laterally to discover a solution.
2. This problem has an unusual solution involving a special move.

For puzzle solutions see page 90.

The opening

Every chess game has an *opening* stage. Both players should have clear plans from the start. In the opening stage, you will have different goals depending on whether you are playing as Black or White.

Opening goals

White plays first and so has a slight advantage in the game. White should try to hold this advantage in the opening stage of the game. Black, coming from behind, should try to end the opening stage at least on an equal footing with white.

All is quiet in the ranks, before battle commences.

Ready to go

Both players should use the opening stage to get into good positions. At the end of this stage, the King should be protected. Pieces should be *developed* (moved into positions to prepare for attack). Take control of the centre by moving your pieces to places where they will dominate as many squares as possible.

Opening blunder

It is perfectly possible for a game to be won or lost in the opening stage. In 1997, IBM's "supercomputer", *Deep Blue*, beat the reigning World Champion, Garry Kasparov, because of a mistake that he made during the opening. He had never been beaten in a match before by a computer.

Television monitors display Kasparov as he takes on his computer opponent, *Deep Blue*.

Do

- Try to control the centre of the board.

- Develop the minor pieces (Knights and Bishops) early on and prepare to use them to attack.

- Move Pawns carefully.*

- Castle as quickly as you safely can.

- Develop your pieces with a plan in mind.

 Don't

- Move pieces more than once at this stage, unless it is part of a plan. Otherwise you will waste time and fall behind in development.

- Sacrifice pieces for no reason at this stage.

- Start attacking too early.

- Expose the Queen to attack.

- Move without thinking – every move counts.

The end of the opening

This board shows how the pieces might be arranged at the end of the opening stage of the game.

Black's pieces are not controlling the centre, but are loitering at the sides, where they are less useful.

White's pieces are well developed at this stage, in a good position to attack in the next stage of the game.

White has used its Pawns to push for central control of this board.

Key words

development Moving pieces during the opening to squares where they will be in useful positions for the battles of the middlegame.

opening The stage between the start of the game and completion of piece development, when the players bring their Pawns and other pieces into play.

Internet link
For a link to a Web site where you can study famous openings in detail, go to **www.usborne-quicklinks.com**

*For more about Pawn structures, see pages 26–27.

Opening sequences

Some distinctive combinations of moves played in the opening stages of chess games are famous and have been given names. Different openings influence what happens later in the game.

Ssshhh...

Naming openings

Opening sequences get their names in different ways:

- Some, like the *Giuoco Piano* (Italian for "quiet game"), get their name from the style of the game that follows the opening.
- Some are named after players, like the Caro-Kann (named after two nineteenth-century German players), or the Ruy Lopez (named after a Spanish priest).
- Others, like the King's Gambit, are named after the move that typifies them.

Each opening sequence tends to have a move that defines it. For example, the Ruy Lopez is defined by White's third move (3. Bb5). After this move, there can be different variations.

The Ruy Lopez opening allows White to carry on with piece development quickly, and then to castle on the Kingside.

Learn from openings

At first it is best to grasp the ideas behind an opening, rather than memorizing a series of moves. When you are playing, your opponent may not always make the moves you expect.

In the opening sequences on the next few pages, try to understand why the players make each move, to improve your own play.

Opening analysis

The only conclusion that experts have so far drawn from analysis of opening sequences seems to be that there is no such thing as the perfect opening!

There have been movements in chess theory in the same way that there have been in music or in art. The *hypermodern** approach, first written about by Aron Nimzowitsch in the 1920s, went against the traditional fight for occupation of the centre of the board. Instead, hypermodernists aimed to control the centre using pieces placed at a distance.

Well, he's wrong if he thinks I'm rushing in with my Pawns...

He can hardly expect me to... I mean, I invented hypermodernism...

Hypermodernists Richard Réti and Aron Nimzowitsch face each other in the Marienbad Tournament in 1925.

Key words

closed game In the opening, a strategy that keeps the attacking pieces behind a strong Pawn structure until the game is in progress.

hypermodernism A movement in chess that started in the 1920s, where a player ignores the usual method of developing pieces to the middle squares, in order to control these squares from a distance.

open game In the opening, a strategy that develops the attacking pieces quickly, positioning them in front of the Pawns.

Early decisions

Your opening moves affect the style of game that follows. If you keep most of your Pawns back and develop other pieces quickly so that they are in front, this is an *open game*. Open games tend to be quite fast and furious, with swift piece exchanges and fighting in the middle of the board.

White and Black have both developed Knights and Bishops to positions in front of their Pawns, opening up lines of attack.

Black has started to build a strong Pawn defence, before advancing any other pieces. This should lead to a *closed game*.

The opposite of this is a *closed game*, where you develop a strong Pawn structure in front and keep the other pieces back until later on.

You can also choose either to push to occupy the middle part of the board or to hang back and wait for your opponent to charge in and – you hope – make mistakes.

Internet link
For a link to a Web site that lists many well-known openings and their defining moves, with a short description of each, go to
www.usborne-quicklinks.com

Did you know?

The game of chess has made regular guest appearances in films and novels over the years. Sometimes the game of chess itself is the star, and sometimes it features as just part of the story.

● *Through the Looking Glass* by Lewis Carroll. Alice steps through the looking glass into a world peopled by strange characters, including giant chess pieces. As she ventures further, she realizes that she is taking part in a giant game of chess.

● *Harry Potter and the Philosopher's Stone* by J.K. Rowling – In their quest to protect the Philosopher's Stone, Harry and his friends Ron and Hermione risk their lives by taking part in a nightmarish game of Wizard Chess.

A still from the movie *Harry Potter and the Philosopher's Stone*, showing Harry and his friends preparing to take part in a giant chess game.

The Italian – *Giuoco Piano*

The Italian opening is also called the *Giuoco Piano*, which means "quiet game" in Italian. However, this is misleading, as it is an opening that can lead to a game full of brutal attacks from both sides and plenty of excitement.

Basic opening strategy

In the Italian opening, White's e-Pawn moves to the centre, and the minor pieces on the Kingside (the Kingside Knights and Bishops) develop quickly, allowing the King to castle. These early moves all fit in with the basic opening techniques that you learn when you start playing chess.

The first move of the Italian opening, (1. e4), is the most common opening move for White, for both new and experienced chess players.

I. e4 e5
These first Pawn moves prepare the way for both sides to get their pieces into play quickly.

2. Nf3 Nc6
The white Knight threatens Black's Pawn. Black defends the Pawn with a Knight of its own.

Internet link
For a link to a Web site where you can find an illustrated variation of the *Giuoco Piano*, go to **www.usborne-quicklinks.com**

How the board looks

With the third move, White launches its Kingside Bishop into the attack, aiming at the f7 Pawn that is defended only by the King. Black mirrors this move with its own Kingside Bishop, and the scene is set for battle to commence!

3. Bc4 Bc5
Let the battle begin!

The pieces are developing symmetrically. Both players have started attacking.

The Pawn on f7 is only protected by the King – this is a defensive weakness.

White's weakness is the Pawn on f2, being attacked by the black Bishop.

What's the idea?

This is an example of an open game. Both White and Black bring their pieces out quickly to seize attacking opportunities – at the same time exposing themselves to the enemy. This means there are likely to be plenty of exciting attacks and exchanges early on in the game. (So much for a "quiet game"!)

The Bishops that enter the battle on each player's third move attack crucial defensive squares, f7 and f2. These squares are weak points in each side's defence, guarded only by the King. Both players need to ensure that the enemy Bishop threat does not lure their King into a deadly trap later on.

The Spanish – Ruy Lopez

The Spanish opening was named after a sixteenth-century Spanish priest called Ruy Lopez. He wrote about his opening strategy in the first known book about chess.

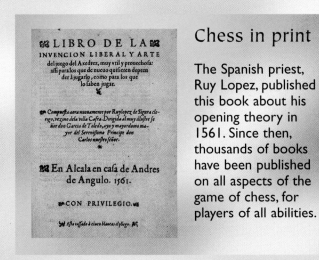

Chess in print

The Spanish priest, Ruy Lopez, published this book about his opening theory in 1561. Since then, thousands of books have been published on all aspects of the game of chess, for players of all abilities.

Answering back

The Spanish opening is also a drive for control of the central squares by White.

1. e4 e5
2. Nf3 Nc6
The first two moves of the Spanish opening are the same as the first two moves of the Italian opening.

White leaps straight into the attack with the third move. Black has to decide how to respond to this attack before it can begin a retaliation. It has a choice of either defence or counter-attack...

Key words

pinned piece A piece that is forced to stay where it is in order to protect another piece.

Bishop on the attack!

3. Bb5
The white Bishop attacks the black Knight.

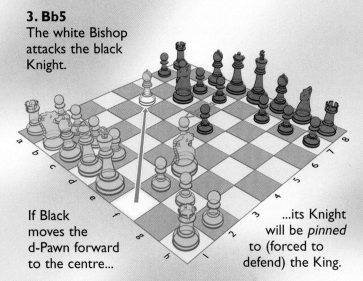

If Black moves the d-Pawn forward to the centre...

...its Knight will be *pinned* to (forced to defend) the King.

The white Bishop on b5 is a threat to Black's defence. This Bishop puts pressure on Black's Knight. If Black moves the d-Pawn (a crucial central Pawn), the Knight will be *pinned*. To move it would leave the Black King in check. (For more about pinned pieces see page 50.)

What happens next?

A common Black counter-attacking response to 3. Bb5 is the following:

3... a6
Black attacks the white Bishop with a Pawn.
4. Bxc6 dxc6
White takes Black's c-file Knight and Black retaliates by taking the white Bishop with its d-Pawn.

A fair exchange?

Here, White loses a Bishop and Black loses a Knight. This is a fair exchange – both pieces are worth three points. Black still has two Bishops, which may be useful to force checkmate later on in the game (see pages 68–69), but also now has doubled Pawns* on the c-file, to White's advantage.

*For more on doubled Pawns, see pages 26–27.

The Queen's Gambit

This opening sequence is characterized by White's second move, which involves a *gambit* – the offer of a Pawn to the opponent, in return for some kind of strategic advantage.

Queenside attack

This opening starts with a White bid for the central squares. Black responds solidly, but White's second move really begins to stir up trouble, in the form of tough decisions to be made early on, for Black.

1. d4 d5
The White and the Black Queenside Pawns advance to meet, head-on, in the middle of the board.

2. c4
This is the crucial move – the gambit. Black now has to decide whether or not to take the white c-Pawn.

Gambits – what's the point?

Playing a gambit in the opening can be positive for two main reasons:

♟ By losing a Pawn, you may open up the board and be able to develop your pieces more quickly than your opponent.

♟ Your opponent, enticed into taking one of your Pawns, may make a change of plan that upsets their strategy.

Offer accepted!

If Black takes the offered white c-Pawn, it will no longer have Pawns on both of the important two central files. This will give White an advantage in the battle for control of the centre.

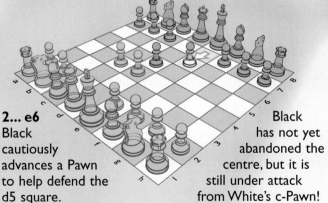

2... dxc4
By taking the white c-Pawn, Black's Pawn moves off a central file.

The black Pawn on c4 is rather weak and White will probably have the chance to take it later in the game.

Offer declined...

If Black does not take the white c-Pawn, that Pawn will continue to threaten the centre. If White takes the black Pawn on d5, it will have a Pawn advantage in the centre and may be able to use this later to undermine Black's Queenside defence.

2... e6
Black cautiously advances a Pawn to help defend the d5 square.

Black has not yet abandoned the centre, but it is still under attack from White's c-Pawn!

Key word

gambit A move made during the opening stage of the game, that offers a Pawn or a minor piece to the opponent, in return for better positions for the remaining pieces.

More White openings...

Once you understand the principles behind the basic opening strategies for White, you can begin to bend the rules to suit how you like to play. The following examples of opening sequences show some different approaches...

The Scandinavian opening

Black responds to White's 1. e4 opening with an immediate Pawn threat.

1. e4 d5
Black makes an aggressive reply to White's opening. But if the white player keeps a cool head, there may not be a problem...

2. exd5 Qxd5
White's Pawn takes the black d-Pawn, only to be taken by the black Queen. But Black's Queen is now developed rather early, and so may be vulnerable to a White attack.

The Four Knights game

Both sides move their pieces symmetrically, to logical positions. Black mirrors White's moves, and the game becomes gradually more tense as each side waits to see who will attack first.

1. e4 e5
2. Nf3 Nc6
3. Nc3 Nf6
After a push for central control, both players develop their Knights to positions where they can defend the Pawns.

Off-the-wall openings

As more and more opening sequences are described, so the need for different names grows. Here are some particularly wacky ones:

Elephant Gambit
Accelerated Dragon
Baby Orang-Utan
Bird's Invitation
Drunken Knight opening
Chameleon Sicilian
Latvian Corkscrew Counter-Gambit
English Double-Whammy
Grunfeld Spike
Hedgehog defence
Hippopotamus
Mad Dog Attack
Woodchuck

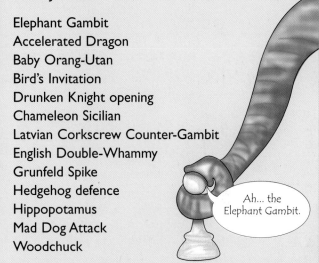

Ah... the Elephant Gambit.

The Reti opening

White's first move is a tricky one for Black to respond to. By not rushing into the centre, the white player does not give away any plans. So, Black moves a Pawn into the centre without delay. White hopes to control the centre from a distance, with pieces rather than Pawns.

1. Nf3 d5
2. c4
White's second move provides a dilemma for Black's d-Pawn. It can either veer off-course to take the white c-Pawn, allow the challenge to stand or push on to d4.

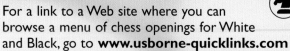

Internet link
For a link to a Web site where you can browse a menu of chess openings for White and Black, go to **www.usborne-quicklinks.com**

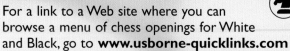

39

The Caro-Kann defence

The Caro-Kann is a defensive opening for Black, which responds to White's opening 1. e4. It builds a solid Pawn structure, while allowing Black's major pieces to escape from the back rank to join the attack.

Let's see White try to get past us...

Rushing for power

Black's aim at the start of the game is to take things at its own pace and build a strong defence, before starting to attack the white Pawns that have rushed into the central part of the board.

1. e4 c6
Black responds to White's move in a laid-back way, choosing not to defend the centre immediately with its d- or e-Pawn, but instead starting to build its own defense.

2. d4 d5
White charges in with its d-Pawn. Black pushes forward to attack the white Pawn on e4, its d-Pawn protected by the Pawn behind it.

3. e5
White advances the e-Pawn. (White could also have advanced a Knight to defend the attacked e-Pawn, or chosen to take the black Pawn on d5.)

Internet link
For a link to a Web site with illustrated variations on the Caro-Kann opening, go to
www.usborne-quicklinks.com

How it looks for Black

Black has already developed a strong Pawn structure, leading up to the centre of the board. White would have to attack the base of this chain (b7) in order to upset these pieces without sacrificing material.

The way Black's Pawns are arranged also allows the Bishop on c8 to escape. However, the b8 Knight is deprived of the square that it would naturally develop to, by the Pawn on c6.

3... Bf5
Black's Queenside Bishop joins the attack...

...and threatens White's c-Pawn.

White's central Pawns are pushing ahead across the board...

...but White must now make sure that it does not fall behind on development as it tries to defend itself.

The fight for control of the centre is raging – but not yet decided one way or the other. The kind of game that follows very much depends on White's next move at this point.

The Sicilian defence

The Sicilian defence has many *variations* (different combinations of moves), leading to games that are open or closed, depending on how White deals with Black's strategies. Some say it is the best opening defence against 1. e4.

A young Bobby Fischer* ponders the best move to make.

Defining moves

The Sicilian defence begins with a distinctive reply by Black to White's first move. This is shown below:

1. e4 c5
Black's first move doesn't threaten the white Pawn on e4. Instead, it looks ahead to White trying to push the other central Pawn to d4. White cannot now do this unchallenged.

Outwit your opponent

A large part of the game of chess involves trying to look ahead and think about what your opponent might do, as well as thinking about the moves that you are going to make as part of your own plan.

As Black, you start off by having to respond to your opponent's opening moves. Black should therefore try to win back the *initiative* in the opening stages of the game. By making a move that dictates what White should or should not do, such as 1... c5, Black can begin to take back some of the control in the game.

Internet link
For a link to a Web site that intoduces some variations on the Sicilian opening at an advanced level, go to **www.usborne-quicklinks.com**

A possible progression...

2. Nf3
White defends a potential white Pawn move to d4.

2... Nc6
Black moves a Knight to attack the same square.

Another possible route...

2. Nf3
White's Knight moves to attack the d4 square.

2... d6
Black builds a defensive Pawn structure.

Key words

initiative Control of the game. The player that is attacking has the initiative.

variation In opening strategy, a variation is a unique combination of moves that belong to a particular type of opening.

*For more about Bobby Fischer, see page 82.

The French defence

Black's pieces emerge slowly in this opening strategy, leaving White free to occupy the centre of the board. Black begins a campaign to undermine this central dominance, by moving either Pawns or Knights to threaten the white Pawns.

Slow and steady

The French defence is a Black response to White's first move, 1. e4. Black builds a solid defence strategy before rushing into the centre.

1. e4 e6
Black responds cautiously to White's central Pawn thrust, choosing to issue no immediate challenge with its own Pawns.

2. d4 d5
Now, with a Pawn on the e-file to provide support from behind, Black can respond with a head-on challenge to White's central Pawns.

The consequences:

♟ Remember – Black's Queenside Bishop will be blocked in during the early stages.

♟ There is likely to be Pawn gridlock in the centre of the board at first.

♟ White will have more space initially; Black should plot to undermine this later.

♟ Usually one player will castle Kingside and the other Queenside in this opening.

What happens next?

In what is called the classic variation, both sides bring in their cavalry (the Knights) to support their clashing Pawns, setting the scene for a fight in the central battleground.

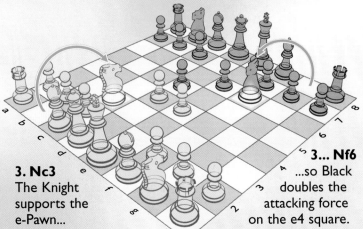

3. Nc3
The Knight supports the e-Pawn...

3... Nf6
...so Black doubles the attacking force on the e4 square.

In the advance variation, White pushes into black territory and locks the central Pawns. To break the deadlock, Black puts pressure on White's d-Pawn with a c-Pawn advance.

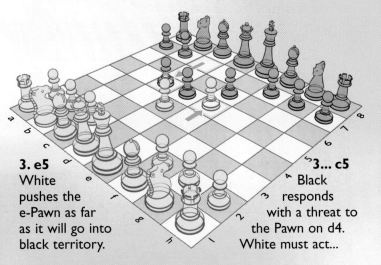

3. e5
White pushes the e-Pawn as far as it will go into black territory.

3... c5
Black responds with a threat to the Pawn on d4. White must act...

Internet link
For a link to a Web site where you can read about the French defence, including an analysis of the Pawn structures that arise, go to **www.usborne-quicklinks.com**

The King's Indian defence

On this page is another opening idea for Black, in response to 1. d4. From a stealthy beginning it can quickly develop into a fierce *counter-attacking* strategy.

Slow and deadly

This opening sequence features what appears to be a fairly restrained series of moves from Black, which conceals the deadly weapon of a *fianchettoed** Bishop, ready to be unleashed on White's unsuspecting central Pawns.

1. d4 Nf6
Black does not rush headlong into the centre with a Pawn, but instead threatens from a distance, using a Knight to prevent White occupying e4.

2. c4 g6
White continues to drive towards the centre; Black quietly moves the g-Pawn forward one square, in preparation for *fianchetto*.

3. Nc3 Bg7
White's Knight moves to defend an anticipated Pawn move to e4. Black completes Kingside *fianchetto*.

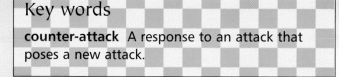

Key words

counter-attack A response to an attack that poses a new attack.

What happens next?

White advances the e-Pawn to the centre, to form a wall of Pawns. Black's d-Pawn moves forward one square, so the Queenside Bishop can get out, preparing for a central challenge.

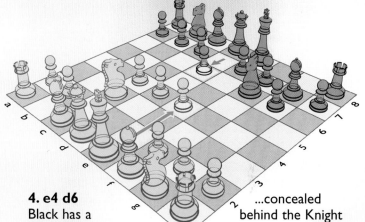

4. e4 d6
Black has a *fianchettoed* Bishop...

...concealed behind the Knight on f6, defending the long a1–h8 diagonal.

One to avoid!

One type of opening to avoid when you are playing as Black is the Scholar's Mate. This sequence of moves could end your chess game embarrassingly quickly if you don't spot it coming!

1. e4 e5
2. Bc4 Bc5
A calm, symmetrical opening, with no apparent threat on either side... but notice that Black's f7 Pawn is only protected by the King.

3. Qh5 Nf6
4. Qf7++ (or Bf7++)
White pounces on Black's weak Pawn, launching a vicious double attack on f7. Black cannot escape – the result is checkmate in only four moves!

*See pages 20–21 for more on the *fianchetto* move.

Thinking in the middlegame

The middlegame begins when both players have brought their pieces into play. Most attacks and exchanges take place during this phase of the game, so try to make sure that you have the upper hand in any ambushes that take place.

Taking charge

The player who is more in control of the game tends to have the *initiative*. The other player has to respond defensively to the attacker's plans instead of getting on with their own plans.

White has the initiative here because he has lots of resources to attack the black King, and Black will have to defend for a number of moves before getting around to his own plans.

Thinking for two

At this stage of the game you should work out what your opponent might do, so that you are less likely to be surprised by an attack.

BOO!

Internet link
For a link to a Web site with some chess rules and guidelines on etiquette for tournament players, go to **www.usborne-quicklinks.com**

Nerves of steel

During the fierce battles of the middlegame, try to remain calm. If you feel that you are doing badly, or even losing the game, you should try not to let your opponent see this.

If you appear to be confident, your opponent might be tricked into believing that you have an amazing plan up your sleeve. If your opponent then makes moves that are more cautious than necessary, you may be able to regain the advantage.

Intimidating opponents

In chess, a lot depends on staying focused and keeping cool. Just imagine trying to do that while playing against either of these:

Aron Nimzowitsch (1886–1935) could be an off-putting adversary. On entering a chess tournament room, he would stand on his head until it was time to start the game. Once he broke his leg during a match by getting it tangled with the leg of his chair.

Nimzowitsch thought of himself as a formidable opponent. His business card described him as "Crown Prince of the Chess World".

Vladimir Kramnik (1975–) has earned the nickname "Iceberg" for his ability to remain cool under great pressure. He claims that part of his success in beating former world champion Garry Kasparov lies in his ability not to be intimidated by him.

Chess etiquette

In chess tournaments, rules govern the way the players behave towards each other. Here are some examples:

● **The "touch-move" rule** If you touch a piece, you must move it. When you have taken your hand away after your move, you must leave the piece where it is.

● **Not saying "check"** It is polite to rely on your opponent noticing.

● **Saying "I adjust"** Say this first if you slightly adjust a piece on its square.

Time factors

If you are playing a friendly game of chess, you will have plenty of time to think about your moves – until your opponent gets bored and decides to do something else, that is!

In a chess competition, time is limited. It is measured using a *chess clock*. The game is lost if a player runs out of time.

Remember that once you touch a piece you are committed to moving it.

Key words

chess clock A special clock with two faces that records the time each player spends on moves in a chess game.

initiative Had by the player who is directing the course of the game by making moves that force certain responses.

Did you know?

After each player has moved four times, there are over 288 billion different possible positions for the pieces on a chess board. So don't feel too frustrated if you can't decide on the right move! Try to narrow down your choices quickly so you only seriously consider two or three.

 Do

● Try to reassess the situation on the board after every move – the balance of power may shift in a short space of time.

● Consider what your opponent is planning as well as thinking of your own strategy.

 Don't

● Allow yourself to get caught out by surprise attacks – keep your eyes peeled for ambushes and traps from every direction.

● Relax – even though things may be going to plan, this can change very quickly!

The board in the middlegame

When you go into the middlegame, your pieces should be well placed if you are to stand a chance in the battle that follows. On these two pages are some examples of good positions and ones to avoid.

Closed or open?

The middlegame (like the opening) can be described as either "open" or "closed".* A closed game has Pawns that are locked together in the middle of the board. An open game has fewer Pawns and so the other pieces are freer to attack each other.

A strong position

This board illustrates a strong position for White in the middlegame.

White's pieces are mobile – they have space and are not blocking each other.

This is an "open" game – few Pawns are left, so other pieces have space to move and attack.

White's Pawns are arranged so that they are not blocking the mobility of White's other pieces too much.

The white player controls more space than Black – its pieces have pushed forwards into its opponent's territory.

Points mean power

The pieces that a player has left on the board are called *material*. The player with the higher total piece value has the *material advantage* – and should have a more powerful army. (How powerful your pieces are also depends on how they are placed on the board.)

Advantage - us!

Mobilizing the troops

In the middlegame you should aim for good piece *mobility* – pieces that are free to move and attack. One way to ensure this is to control as much space as possible, so that the pieces have room to move. Remember though, that you will have to work to defend the space you control.

*For more about closed and open games, see page 35.

Too much responsibility

In your drive to obliterate your opponent's defence, it helps if you can exploit any weaknesses that you spot. For example, your opponent may have a piece that is working to defend more than one other piece. This is an *overloaded piece*, and it is a weakness. If it moves to defend a piece, it will leave another undefended.

I don't know what to do!

Internet link
For a link to a Web site providing general advice on the middlegame, go to **www.usborne-quicklinks.com**

Did you know?

Some chess games are over well before the middlegame... the quickest checkmate of all only takes two moves!

A weak position

This board illustrates a weak position for Black in the middlegame.

Black has a bad Pawn structure. There are two pairs of doubled Pawns on the c- and f-files.

Black's pieces have poor mobility, so Black is less able to launch an effective attack.

White's Rooks are well placed on the middle two files. From here, it can launch effective attacks using these pieces.

White has a material disadvantage, but it has better mobility than Black and so is more likely to win at this point.

Vulnerable King

Can I stay here?

Your King may look well defended, if you castled* during the opening and it is tucked behind a wall of Pawns. But during the middlegame there are still many powerful, dangerous pieces on the board. Be vigilant and defend your King at all times.

*For more about castling, see page 13.

Key words

material The pieces that are left on the board.

material advantage/disadvantage Having pieces of a greater/lesser value than the enemy's.

mobility The ability of pieces to move freely.

overloaded piece A piece that has more than one defensive job to do, leaving it (or the pieces it is defending) open to attack.

Middlegame puzzles

The middlegame is a battlefield, where you need to keep one eye on your attacking chances and the other firmly fixed on your own King's defences. Watch out for sneaky ways to deliver an early checkmate to your opponent.

Did you know?

Some people study "fairy chess" problems, using board positions that could not arise in a normal game. They may also feature extra, made-up pieces, with special moves.

Internet link
For a link to a Web site with more chess puzzles, go to **www.usborne-quicklinks.com**

The right move

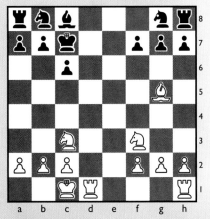

Can you spot the most devastating move for White to make here?

CLUE: The black King should watch his back!

Well-placed piece

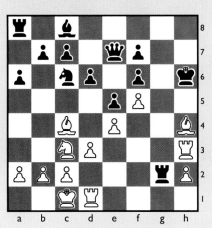

How can White use two pieces at once to annihilate the black King?

CLUE: Find a mobile attacking piece and use it.

Nowhere to run

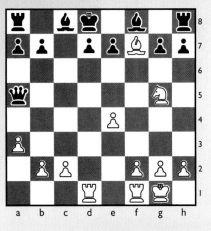

All looks calm here, but can you see how White can finish off the black King?

CLUE: How can you block the black King's escape?

Two-move mate

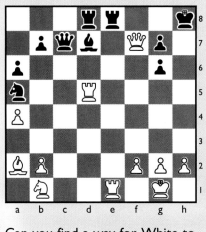

Can you find a way for White to give checkmate in two moves?

CLUE: Consider making a sacrifice.

For puzzle solutions see page 90.

♔ Defending the King

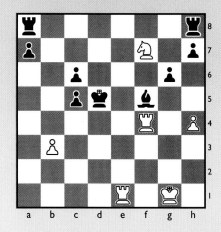

(1) It might seem as if the black King has plenty of escape options, but can you see how White can use its pieces to trap it in checkmate?

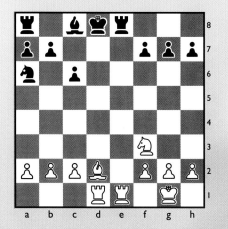

(2) How can the white player here make the most of Black's vulnerable uncastled King, and force checkmate with only one move?

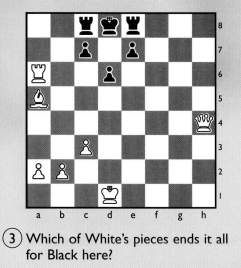

(3) Which of White's pieces ends it all for Black here?

For puzzle solutions see pages 90–91.

CLUES:
1. Your Rooks need to support each other.

2. Use a double check to give mate.

3. Which of White's three pieces can attack at close range without risk?

♙ Square overload

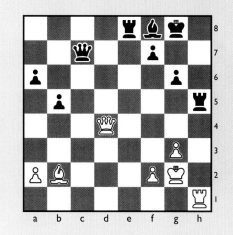

Can White checkmate in two moves?

CLUE:
Exploit the overloaded square, h8.

♙ Noble sacrifice

How can a White sacrifice be used to give mate in two moves?

CLUE:
Lose the Queen!

♙ Deadly initiative

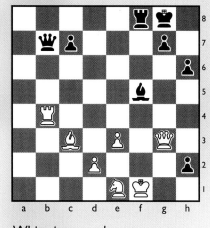

White is powerless to escape mate. Can you see Black's move?

CLUE:
Go for a double check.

Tactical tricks

Try using these tactical tricks to outwit your enemy. The objective of each is to unleash an attack so cunning and deadly that there is no way your opponent can escape without losing pieces.

Pinned down

An attack on a piece that is shielding a piece of greater value is called a *pin*. The *pinned piece* must stay where it is until the piece that is attacking it moves or is captured. If the pinned piece moves, it will leave the more valuable piece behind open to capture.

The white Bishop is attacking the Black Knight. If the Knight moves, it will expose the black Queen.

Black's Knight is an example of a pinned piece in this illustration.

Skewered!

A *skewer* is a kind of reverse pin. It is an attack on a valuable piece, that forces that piece to move. When this valuable piece moves, it exposes another, less valuable piece behind, to be attacked and captured.

As with the pin, the defending player is bound to lose a piece one way or the other, and can only act to limit the damage. (For information on defending against pins and skewers, see page 58.)

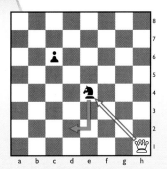

1... Nd2
Black's Knight moves swiftly away from an attack by the white Queen, leaving a black Pawn vulnerable.

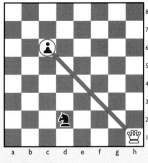

2. Qxc6
With no other pieces left defending it, the isolated black Pawn makes easy pickings for the white Queen.

Two-pronged attack

A *fork* is an attack on two or more pieces at the same time by a single enemy piece. The player that is under this double attack usually has no way of avoiding a capture. Its irregular move makes the Knight a good forking piece.

White's pieces both fall victim to Black's Knight fork, though they are not on the same rank, file or diagonal.

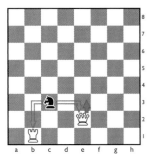

1. Qe3
Black's Knight forks White's Rook and Queen. The Queen escapes and attacks the Knight...

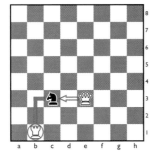

1... NxRb1
...but Black can now take White's Rook with its Knight and evade the Queen's attack.

Tactic tip

Look for ways to use your Knights to fork your opponents, who will be powerless to stop the attack by blocking a Knight's way with pieces. The Knight can simply leap over them! Its irregular jumping move also makes it hard for your opponent to see it coming in for such an attack.

Internet link
For a link to a Web site with more illustrated examples of pins, skewers and forks, go to **www.usborne-quicklinks.com**

Concealed threat

When one piece is moved to reveal an attack by another piece lurking behind, this is called a *discovered attack*. A discovered attack might take your opponent by surprise so that they do not see the threat until it is too late.

If the black Bishop moves, it will reveal a discovered attack on the white Queen from the black Rook.

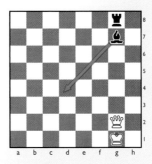

1... Bd4+
Black's Bishop moves to reveal a discovered attack on the white Queen by the Rook.

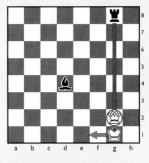

2. Kf1 Rxg2
The white King must move out of check, so Black's Rook is free to take the white Queen.

Key words

discovered attack A piece moves to reveal another attack from a different piece.
fork A simultaneous attack on two or more pieces by one enemy piece. Only one piece can escape the attack – the other will be captured.
pin An attack on a piece that is shielding one of greater value.
pinned piece A piece that must stay still to protect another piece of greater value.
skewer An attack that forces a valuable piece to move, exposing one of less value to attack.

Tactical trick puzzles

To solve the puzzles on these two pages you will need to use tactical moves like forks, pins and skewers to win important pieces from your opponent and even give checkmate. Watch out – some of the puzzles are quite tricky!

Did you know?

Until the beginning of last century, it was a rule that you had to announce a check. The rule was that if you didn't announce a check, it didn't count.

Internet link

For a link to a Web site with more chess puzzles, go to **www.usborne-quicklinks.com**

♟ Slice the defence

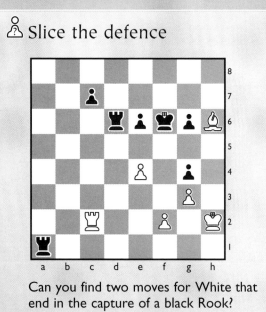

Can you find two moves for White that end in the capture of a black Rook?

CLUE: Fork the King, then skewer it!

♟ Lethal weapon

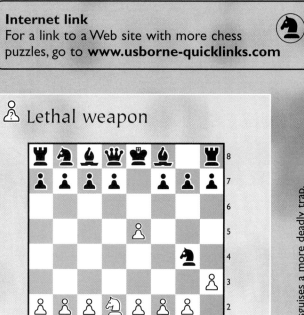

The black Knight must move – how can Black turn this into a three-move mate?

CLUE: A Queen fork disguises a more deadly trap.

♟ Don't get pinned down

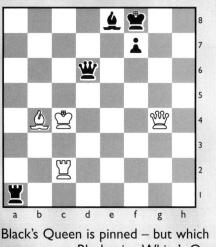

Black's Queen is pinned – but which moves mean Black wins White's Queen?

CLUE: Escape a pin to set up a skewer.

♟ Cutlery crusade

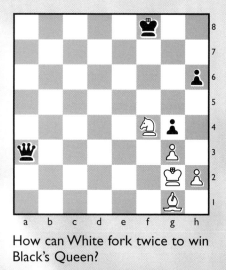

How can White fork twice to win Black's Queen?

CLUE: The black King and Queen share a diagonal.

For puzzle solutions see page 90.

♟ Protected Pawn

Black's Pawn hopes to promote. How can Black ensure the Pawn's safety?

CLUE: Sacrifice a piece to disable White's Rook.

♟ Forked lightning

Can you find a two-move combination for White to take the black Rook?

CLUE: Plan to fork Black's Rook and King.

♟ Rook revenge

Can you see two moves for White that win a Rook?

CLUE: Ditch the passed Pawn and skewer the King.

♟ Widen the gap

White can win the Queen (and ultimately the game) here – how?

CLUE: Try to set up a Knight fork.

♟ Battle of the Bishops

How can White checkmate Black in two moves here?

CLUE: Two words – "Queen" and "sacrifice".

♟ Inevitable capture

How can White guarantee winning a major piece with its next move?

CLUE: Get the King on one prong of your fork!

For puzzle solutions see page 90.

Making plans

If you want to get the edge on your opponent in a game of chess, you need to make every single move count. To ensure this, the moves that you make during a game should all be part of a *plan*.

Aims and objectives

To make a plan, you need to decide on what you want to achieve. Your plan will probably depend on what stage of the game you are at. Examples of plans include exchanging pieces, promoting a Pawn or checkmating your opponent.

1. b7 Qd8
2. b8(Q)
White's plan here was simple – to promote a Pawn. Black moved the Queen to attack the queening square, but White had planned for this and had back-up in the form of a Rook on b1.

Using tempo

The number of moves it takes you to achieve a particular aim is important in chess. You should try to be ahead in piece development and the race for occupation of territory on the board.

A *tempo* is a chess unit equal to a single move. A player loses a tempo by wasting a move – for example by using two moves to get a piece to a position that it could have reached in one move. If several moves are wasted, the player loses *tempi*. (The other player gains tempi.)

You may choose to lose a tempo*, to stall for time or to wrongfoot your opponent.

*For more about losing a tempo, see page 14.

Pole position

Your plan might be to improve your general *position*. A simple way to assess your position is to count the number of squares that your pieces could safely attack. If your pieces have more attacking scope than your opponent's, then you probably have a positional advantage.

The Black player has a positional advantage here. The blue shaded areas show all the squares that it could safely attack. The red shaded areas show all the squares White can safely attack.

Target weaknesses

One way to decide on a plan is to look for weaknesses in your enemy's army. Some examples of weaknesses that you could choose to exploit include a weak Pawn structure (where Pawns are undefended or blocking the movement of other pieces) or an exposed King.

Here, Black has an isolated Pawn on the d-file. White can make a plan to take this Pawn, leaving the way clear for its own d-Pawn to advance.

Playing chess in a school chess club is a good way to practise and improve your skills.

An attacking plan for White

On this board, White has the positional advantage and should plan attacks on Black. (Black should plan to weaken this advantage.)

♙ Dominant central Pawns that can be used to hold off Black attacks on the centre.

♙ A Queenside Pawn majority that can advance and attack, while the Kingside Pawns defend.

♙ A passed Pawn on the a-file, approaching its queening square. White should try to protect and ultimately promote this Pawn.

♙ A well-protected King. White has guarded against the King being trapped on the back rank by moving the h-Pawn forward one square.

A defensive plan for Black

On this board, Black is at a disadvantage and should plan to improve on the situation. (White's plan should exploit these weaknesses.)

♟ Captured Pawns on the Kingside. Black should bolster its defence on this side with other pieces to stop White promoting Pawns.

♟ Doubled Pawns on the c-file, that either need defending by other pieces, or may be sacrificed to open up better positions for Black.

♟ An isolated Pawn on the a-file. Black will need to defend this Pawn using other pieces.

♟ A King that has not yet castled to safety. Black should plan to castle Queenside soon.

 Do

● Look for easy targets to exploit.

● Rectify weaknesses in your own position as quickly as you can.

● If you can't see anything more obvious to aim for, you could try to control more space, or create passed Pawns.

Don't

● Continue to pursue a plan if it doesn't work. Be flexible.

● Forget to foil your opponent's plans!

Key words

plan A series of moves designed to achieve a particular goal, for example to promote a Pawn.

position A measure of the amount of attacking control that you have over the squares on the board.

tempo (plural tempi) A unit of time in chess – equivalent to a single move.

Internet link
For a link to a Web site where you can find out more about the idea of tempo as it is used to measure time in chess games, with illustrated examples, go to
www.usborne-quicklinks.com

Combination puzzles

During the game, you should be on the lookout for clever combinations of moves that will deliver checkmate. Use tactical tricks and force checks to trap a vulnerable King, maybe even forcing it into a checkmate position.

Did you know?
Castling was originally two moves (first the King, then the Rook). It became one single move in 1561. You can still castle in two moves – called "castling by hand".

Internet link
For a link to a Web site with more chess puzzles, go to www.usborne-quicklinks.com

♙ Checkmate surprise

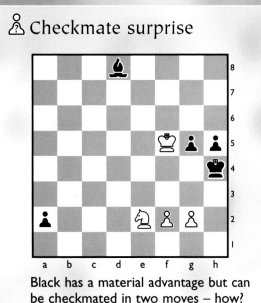

Black has a material advantage but can be checkmated in two moves – how?

CLUE:
Make a cunning Knight move.

♙ Weak spot

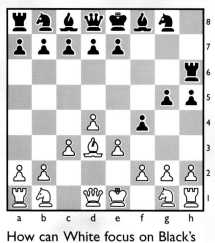

How can White focus on Black's weaknesses to force mate in two?

CLUE:
Make a major sacrifice.

♙ Push for victory

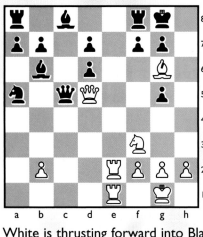

White is thrusting forward into Black territory – how does it mate in two?

CLUE:
Build a back rank trap.

♙ Wrongfooted Rooks

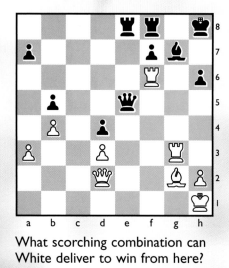

What scorching combination can White deliver to win from here?

CLUE:
How can you keep the King trapped where it is?

For puzzle solutions see pages 90–91.

♟ Tragedy for the King

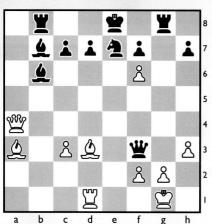

Find a winning combination for White featuring a sacrifice and a double check.

CLUE: Use a sacrifice to draw the King out to a vulnerable square.

♟ Inevitable defeat

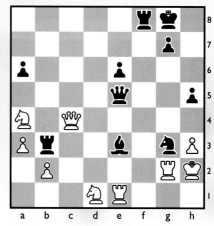

Black can sacrifice here to mate in four moves – what are they?

CLUE: In all three solutions, a Bishop makes the first move.

♟ Spoilt for choice

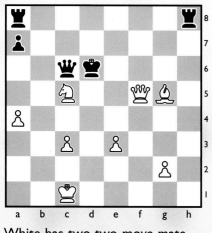

White has two two-move mate options here – can you find them?

CLUE: In both cases, White's Queen is all-important.

♟ Humble mate

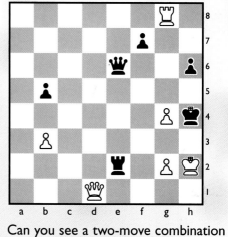

Can you see a two-move combination for White to give checkmate here?

CLUE: Release the white Pawns from the pin first.

♟ Early mate

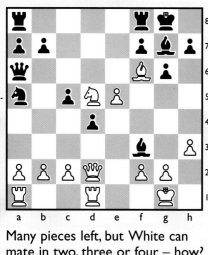

Many pieces left, but White can mate in two, three or four – how?

CLUE: The first move is crucial to all three solutions.

♟ Long-term goal

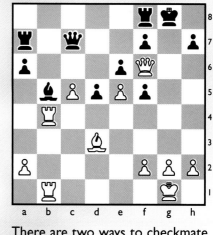

There are two ways to checkmate in four here – can you find them?

CLUE: Both solutions require a Rook sacrifice.

For puzzle solutions see pages 90–91.

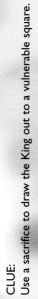

Defence techniques

The best way to win a chess game is to seize the initiative and be the attacker. But there will be times when you need to play defensively, in response to an attack from your opponent.

Don't get pinned down

To avoid any of your valuable pieces being pinned* or skewered* by your opponent, be careful if two undefended pieces occupy the same rank, file or diagonal. In this kind of position they are most vulnerable to one of these types of attack.

1. Nd2
Here, White can pin the black Knight to the Queen on the next move by moving the Knight on f3. The Knight will not be able to move, until the Queen has moved away.

Watch out for forks

Forks* are quite tricky to guard against. The only way is to keep a very close eye on your opponent's attacking pieces, especially the Knights. The Knight's unusual move makes it difficult to see when it comes in for a fork attack. Because it can jump, it is also hard to defend against, as you cannot deter it by placing pieces to block its way.

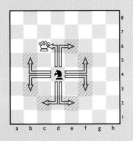

The Knight attacking the Queen could also attack another piece on any of the shaded squares.

Caught in a trap

If you find that you are the victim of a pin, fork or skewer, all is not lost. There are two things you can do to limit the damage:

● You could try to distract your opponent by launching an attack of your own on a different part of the board. While your opponent responds to this, you may have time to bring in reinforcements to defend the pieces that are under fire.

● Whatever kind of trap you are caught in, you will probably have to move a piece away from an immediate threat. By doing so, you will leave another piece exposed to attack. To limit the damage as much as possible, try to move the first piece to a place where it can defend the second piece, as in the examples below:

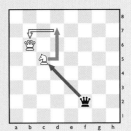

1. Nd7
The pinned white Knight moves, exposing the white Queen, but defending it at the same time. Black cannot capture the white Queen without losing its own.

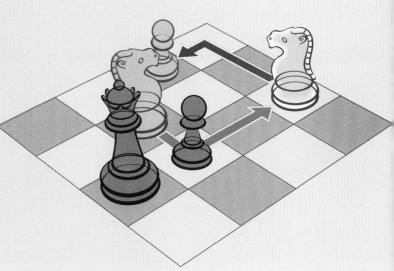

If you are caught in a skewer, try to move one of the attacked pieces away to a square from where it can defend the other attacked piece.

*For more about forks, pins and skewers, see pages 50–51.

Evade the Scholar's Mate

Checkmate in four moves, (Scholar's Mate*), spells doom for the unwary. Your opponent may disguise this deadly move sequence by adding extra moves, but if you know the danger signs you will be able to take evasive action before it is too late.

Scholar's Mate uses a double attack on the white f2 Pawn or the black f7 Pawn, by the Kingside Bishop and the Queen. If your opponent mobilizes both this Bishop and the Queen during the opening, you should be suspicious.

To defend against checkmate in this situation, you can do either of the following:

● Move your Knight to f6 (or f3) – this is a strong position for your Knight in the next stage of the game.

● Protect the f7 square at all costs – for example by moving your Queen to e7. Or block the White Queen's attack with a Pawn move to g6.

Danger for Black! White mounts a combined Bishop and Queen attack on the f7 square.

Defensive approach

Aron Nimzowitsch liked to play strategically in chess games. He used a technique called *overprotection*, which means that certain squares (for example the crucial central square e5) are heavily defended by several pieces.

This meant that any attack his opponent dared to launch on the e5 square would be quickly annihilated. Any of the defending pieces would also be able to carry out other duties elsewhere on the board at any time without leaving the square undefended.

This board illustrates one of Nimzowitsch's (playing White) favourite concepts – overprotection of the e5 square by a Bishop, a Knight and the Queen.

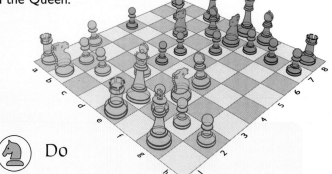

Do

● Be on the lookout for tactical traps like pins, forks and skewers.

● Defend aggressively – if your opponent attacks, do what they least expect and attack back.

Don't

● Panic... If you are caught in a trap, it may be possible to limit the damage or even turn the situation to your own advantage.

Internet link
For a link to a Web site where you can find a chess glossary that describes the idea of overprotection simply and effectively, go to **www.usborne-quicklinks.com**

Key words
overprotection Defence of a square by more than one piece, making an attack on that square difficult for the opponent.

*For more about Scholar's Mate, see page 43.

Sacrifice puzzles

Sometimes you will find you have to lose material to get ahead in a game of chess. Can you see how, in the puzzles on these two pages, you can force checkmate in either two or three moves by making a well-timed sacrifice?

Did you know?

The World Chess Federation estimates that there are at least 550 million people worldwide who play chess.

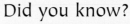

Internet link
For a link to a Web site with more chess puzzles, go to
www.usborne-quicklinks.com

Seal Black's fate

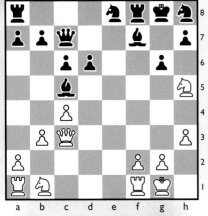

Sacrifice a piece to give mate on White's second move.

CLUE: How can you bury the King?

Building a wall

How can White sacrifice a piece to allow the Queen to deliver checkmate?

CLUE: Make sure you move the right piece or all is lost!

Sacrificial barrage

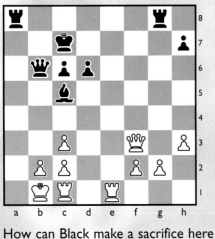

How can Black make a sacrifice here and mate on the second move?

CLUE: Make White's piled up Pawns work against the King.

King-baiting

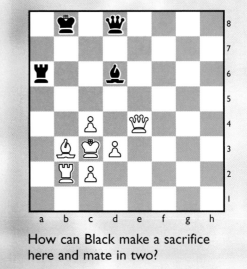

How can Black make a sacrifice here and mate in two?

CLUE: Try to draw the King towards a line of attack.

For puzzle solutions see page 91.

60

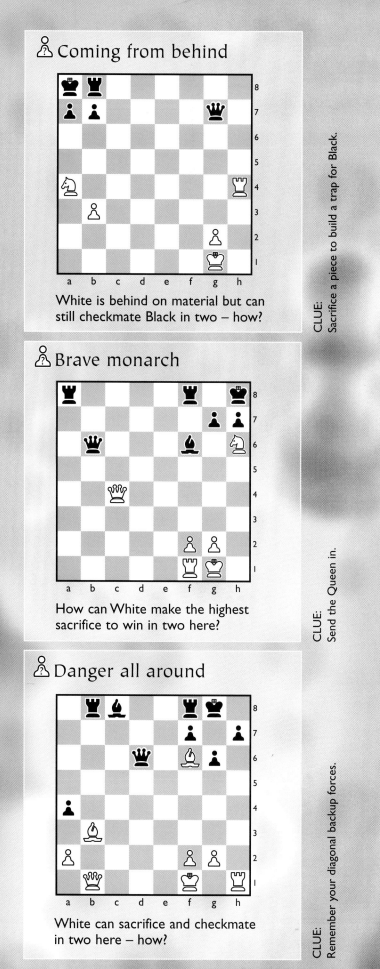

♟ Coming from behind

White is behind on material but can still checkmate Black in two – how?

CLUE: Sacrifice a piece to build a trap for Black.

♟ Piledriver

How can White sacrifice to force the loss of Black's Queen and checkmate?

CLUE: Dive straight to the heart of the black defence.

♟ Brave monarch

How can White make the highest sacrifice to win in two here?

CLUE: Send the Queen in.

♟ Wriggling free

How can Black promote a Pawn and checkmate from this position?

CLUE: Make a sacrifice count by delivering check.

♟ Danger all around

White can sacrifice and checkmate in two here – how?

CLUE: Remember your diagonal backup forces.

♟ Closing in

How can White use a sacrifice to mate in three here?

CLUE: Consider how Black must respond to what you do.

For puzzle solutions see page 91.

The endgame

The endgame is the stage when both players have lost most of their pieces, leaving the board fairly empty. Not all chess games reach this stage; sometimes the game ends in checkmate during the middlegame or even the opening.

More responsibility

In the endgame, you should use your King as an attacking piece. Your opponent now has fewer pieces left with which to threaten your King, so it can move around more. You also have fewer pieces left to attack your enemy, so you need to make full use of them all.

The King may not be able to move far, but it can attack eight squares at once.

Ambitious Pawns

Pawns become more valuable later in the game. This is because at this stage, the race for Pawn promotion* is really on. Promoting just one Pawn to a Queen is usually enough to tip the balance in your favour and enable you to win the game.

Ha ha! Power at last...

Keeping the pieces

During the endgame, it becomes vitally important that the few pieces that you do have left work together, providing support for each other without getting in each other's way.

For example, if you have a white-squared Bishop and a smattering of Pawns, try to keep the Pawns on black squares, to give the Bishop maximum freedom of movement (making it a good Bishop**).

As a general rule, try to keep your pieces near the centre of the board, on *open lines*, where they can function at full power.

White is in a good position in this endgame, with a good Bishop, passed Pawns under the watchful eye of the King, and a mobile Rook.

A square fit for a Queen

A square a Pawn needs to reach to gain promotion is called a *queening square*. You should use your pieces to help your own Pawns to reach their queening squares safely.

Don't forget, though, to try to stop your opponent from promoting Pawns at the same time.

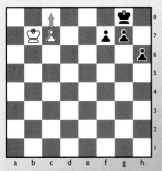

1. c8(Q)+
The white Pawn reaches its queening square. Black's King was too far away to have prevented this and cannot capture this dangerous new Queen.

1... Kh7
The position of White's newly promoted Queen means that Black has to move the King. (If Black hadn't left the h7 square clear, this would have been back-rank mate.)

Key words

queening square The square on the far side of the board that a Pawn needs to reach to gain promotion (usually to a Queen).

open lines Ranks, files or diagonals that are clear of pieces.

Typical endgame

In the most common type of endgame each player has a King, a Rook and a few Pawns left. Make sure that your Rook is on an open file where it has as much influence as possible, or on a file behind a passed Pawn, to act as a bodyguard until the Pawn can promote.

In the example below, Black and White have almost identical positions, apart from the two Rooks.

White's Rook ties Black's to the defence of the f7 Pawn and also keeps the black King cut off on the back rank. Black's Rook, by contrast, has no mobility. It is behind a locked Pawn and blocked by a Pawn on the same rank.

Internet link
For a link to a Web site where you can find out more about useful strategies to use in the endgame, go to **www.usborne-quicklinks.com**

 Do

● Use the King. In the endgame it can be a vital attacking piece.

● Guard your passed Pawns carefully. They are valuable and you should do everything you can to try to promote them.

 Don't

● Allow your opponent to promote Pawns or you will be at a disadvantage.

● Let your pieces get blocked in so you can't use them to their full attacking potential.

Endgame puzzles

When the game enters its final stage, you need to make all your remaining pieces work hard together to deliver checkmate. These endgame puzzles will test your ability to construct a trap, or mating net, using the material you have left.

Internet link
For a link to a Web site where you can find more chess puzzles, go to **www.usborne-quicklinks.com**

Mate surprise

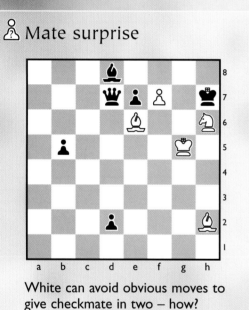

White can avoid obvious moves to give checkmate in two – how?

CLUE: The solution is not a Queen capture or Pawn promotion.

Cavalry charge

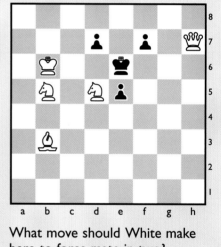

What move should White make here to force mate in two?

CLUE: The best move is not a direct attack.

Sticky end

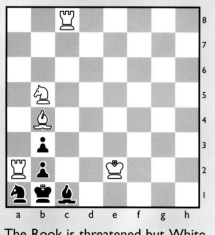

The Rook is threatened but White can still give checkmate in two – how?

CLUE: Remember – Black is moving down the board.

King pressure

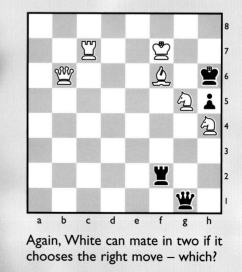

Again, White can mate in two if it chooses the right move – which?

CLUE: Move a piece into position to close the mating net.

For puzzle solutions see page 91.

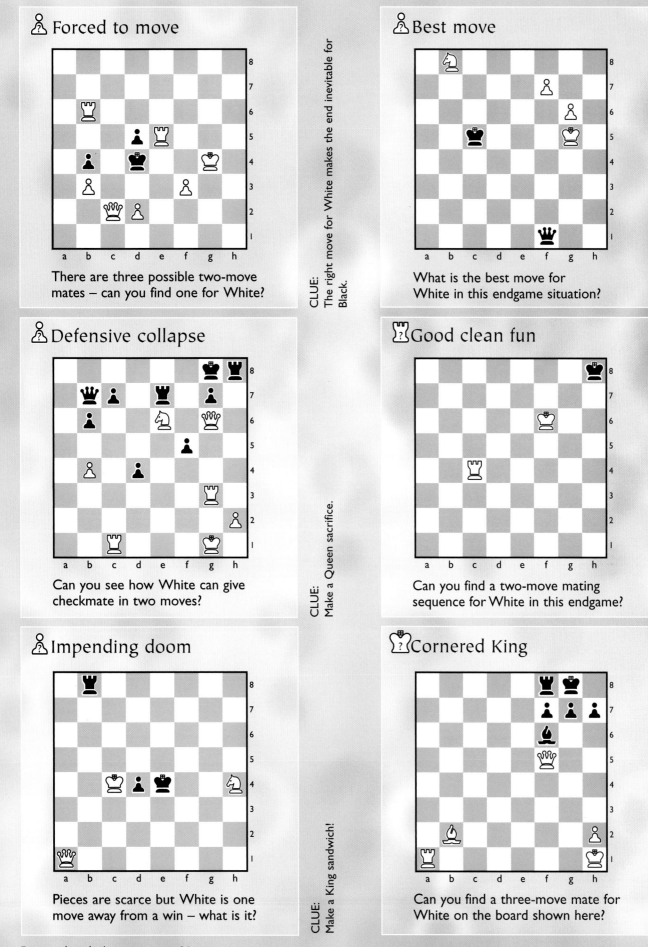

♟ Forced to move

There are three possible two-move mates – can you find one for White?

CLUE:
The right move for White makes the end inevitable for Black.

♟ Best move

What is the best move for White in this endgame situation?

CLUE:
Don't give Black a chance to move its Queen.

♟ Defensive collapse

Can you see how White can give checkmate in two moves?

CLUE:
Make a Queen sacrifice.

♜ Good clean fun

Can you find a two-move mating sequence for White in this endgame?

CLUE:
Don't let the King wriggle free.

♟ Impending doom

Pieces are scarce but White is one move away from a win – what is it?

CLUE:
Make a King sandwich!

♚ Cornered King

Can you find a three-move mate for White on the board shown here?

CLUE:
Make a sacrifice to clear lines of attack for your pieces.

For puzzle solutions see page 91.

Attacking the King

An attack on the King is called *check*. Putting the enemy King in check does not mean you will definitely win the game, but it does mean that your opponent is forced to get out of check before making any other moves.

Take action

You must take evasive action if your King is in check. There are three ways to get out of check:

- Capture the checking piece.
- Place one of your own pieces between the checking piece and your King. (This will not work if the checking piece is a Knight.)
- Move your King away from the attack.

If you can't do any of these, it is checkmate.

Here, the white King is in check, but White has four options available – so all is not lost yet! Can you see what they are*?

> **Internet link**
> For a link to a Web site where you can see an animation that illustrates perpetual check, go to **www.usborne-quicklinks.com**

Sneaky checking

Your opponent might not see check coming if it is in the form of *discovered check* – when you move one of your pieces to reveal a piece behind that is giving check.

1. Bc7+
The white Bishop's move reveals a discovered check from the Rook. The black King will have to move out of check...

1... Kh8
2. Bxa5
The King moves, disastrously leaving the white Queen exposed to capture by the white Bishop.

Sneakier checking

An even nastier surprise for your opponent is *double check* – when you move one piece into position to give check, revealing another checking piece behind.

If your King is double checked, you will have to move it. Taking one of the checking pieces with another of your pieces will not be enough. If you cannot move your King, you will be checkmated.

1. Ng6++
At first glance, Black seems to have a huge advantage. But one move from White gives double check from which there is no escape – so it is checkmate.

*Bxe3, Ne2, Kd1 or Kf1.

Forced moves

When you have to make a move, even though that move will put you in a worse position, this is known as *zugzwang* (German for "forced to move"). In this example, Black is in a *zugzwang* position that leads directly to checkmate by White.

Please don't make me do that...

1... h2
2. Nf2++
Black has no choice but to advance the h-Pawn. (The King cannot move to a safe square.) When the white Knight moves, Black's King is checkmated.

Slippery customer

When a player is put in check repeatedly, but cannot be checkmated, this is called *perpetual check*. This is a draw* – both sides can move but there is no way of resolving the situation.

1. Nf7+ Kg8
White was just about to be checkmated here (1... Qa3), but moves to put the black King in check.

2. Nh6+ Kh8
Black is in perpetual check. The Knight and the King could move back and forth forever – this is draw.

Did you know?

In a chess match between Crouch and Britton in the UK in 1984, Black gave check 43 times on consecutive turns!

The most checks recorded in a single match was 141, in a match between Johnsen and Gausdal in 1991. White gave check 100 times; Black 41 times. After all that, the game ended in draw.

♕ Do

● Give check as a means of forcing your opponent to move. By moving, your opponent may lose time or neglect other pieces – and you can exploit this as part of a plan.

♚ Don't

● Give check unnecessarily. It may make you feel powerful, but should only be done as part of a plan.

● Say "check" if you are playing in a chess competition. It is good manners to let your opponent notice this.

● Accidentally put your opponent in a perpetual check if you want to win the game – but it's fine if you want to draw.

Key words

check An attack on the King.

discovered check When a piece moves to reveal a piece behind that is giving check.

double check When a piece moves to give check, revealing a checking piece behind.

perpetual check When a player is checked repeatedly but cannot be checkmated – a draw.

zugzwang A situation where you are forced to move, even if there is no good move to make.

*For more about drawn games, see pages 72–73.

The King is dead – checkmate

Checkmating your opponent is the ultimate goal at the start of any game of chess. You may be able to force checkmate at any stage of the game. The examples on these two pages deal with checkmate in the endgame.

Playing to win

The endgame examples on these two pages show combinations of pieces with enough power to win. If your pieces don't have enough power the result will be a draw. (For more about drawn games see pages 72–73.)

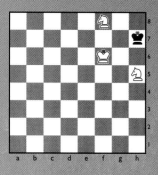

Two Knights and a King do not have enough combined force to give checkmate.

Using the opposition

Stay out of my way!

If there is one square between your King and your opponent's after your move, you have the opposition* – the opposing King cannot move closer. Use the opposition to keep the King at the edge while your other pieces trap it.

Internet link
For a link to a Web site where you can find out more about checkmating patterns, go to **www.usborne-quicklinks.com**

*For more about the opposition, see page 14.

Royal couple

It is fairly straightforward to checkmate a lone King with a King and a Queen. You will need to use them as a team, though. Try to drive the enemy King to a rank or file at the edge of the board. Use your own King to hold it there while you go in for the kill with the Queen. The Queen can sweep in to checkmate the King along a rank, file or diagonal.

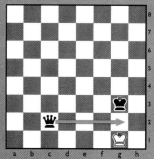

1... Qf1++
The black King holds the white King on the back rank, while the black Queen swoops in to give checkmate.

1... Qg2++
This time the black King keeps the white King still for the Queen to slide in from the side to give checkmate.

Rook and King v. King

It is also possible to checkmate your opponent using only one Rook and your King. The principle is similar to using your Queen – the only difference is that of course the Rook cannot sweep in for the kill along a diagonal in the same way that your Queen can. Again, you will need to use your King as part of your trap or *mating net*, as this example shows.

1... Ra1++
The black King holds the white King on the back rank, using the power of the opposition, while the black Rook glides in to seal the white King's fate.

Powerful pair

Two Rooks are powerful enough to force checkmate. Use them together to inch the enemy King to an edge rank or file, where it will be completely blockaded by the two Rooks.

1. Ra8++
The black King is held on the back rank by the white Rook on the seventh rank, making it easy pickings for the other white Rook.

King and two Bishops v. King

Checkmate is more difficult with two Bishops and a King. You need to force the enemy King into a corner, and limit its movement using your King. The two Bishops together form a line of fire that it can't cross.

1. Bd5++
White's King is cornered by the glowering black King and the twin searchlights of the Bishop pair.

Mixed army

Push your opponent's King into a *dangerous corner* (the same colour as your remaining Bishop) if all you have is a King, a Knight and a Bishop against a lone King. It might prove quite difficult to get your pieces arranged to produce checkmate – but it is possible!

1. Be6++
The white King traps Black's King on the back rank. A Knight stops its sideways movement. When the white Bishop attacks, the black King has nowhere left to run – checkmate.

 Do

- Keep your King and minor pieces together for safety if they are all you have left.

- Use Bishops or Rooks together if you have both, to form a barrier that a King cannot cross.

Don't

- Leave your King to cope on its own – if it becomes isolated it will be more vulnerable.

- Allow your opponent to get his King to a square where it will be safe from attack, or you will be unable to checkmate and will have to settle for a draw.

If you only have your King left, you will not be able to win but you may still be able to escape being checkmated.

Key words

dangerous/non-dangerous corner
The corner square on which a King is exposed to/safe from the opposing Bishop.

mating net Pieces placed in such a way that wherever the enemy King moves, it will be trapped.

Checkmate puzzles

Most chess puzzles involve trying to give checkmate in a certain number of moves. By practising these kinds of puzzle, you should improve your ability to spot checkmate opportunities that occur in your own games.

Walled-in King

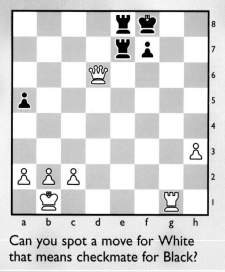

Can you spot a move for White that means checkmate for Black?

CLUE: Attack the King's exposed side – it can't run away.

Surrounded

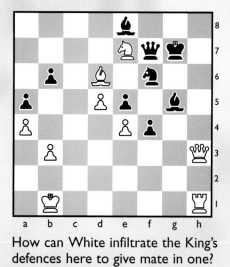

How can White infiltrate the King's defences here to give mate in one?

CLUE: Surround the black King with attacking pieces.

Discovered doom

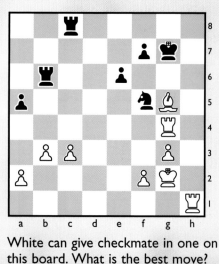

White can give checkmate in one on this board. What is the best move?

CLUE: Reveal a Rook.

Humble attacker

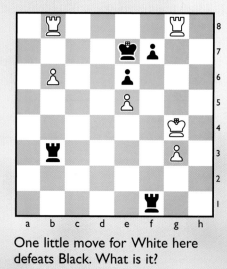

One little move for White here defeats Black. What is it?

CLUE: Use a Pawn as part of your mating net.

For puzzle solutions see page 91.

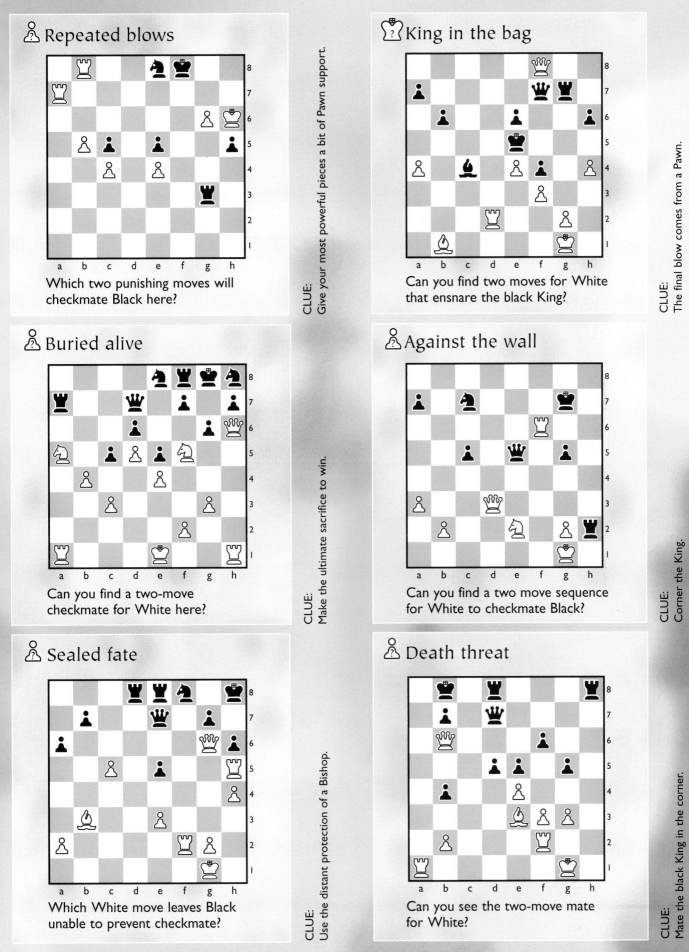

♟ Repeated blows

Which two punishing moves will checkmate Black here?

CLUE: Give your most powerful pieces a bit of Pawn support.

♚ King in the bag

Can you find two moves for White that ensnare the black King?

CLUE: The final blow comes from a Pawn.

♟ Buried alive

Can you find a two-move checkmate for White here?

CLUE: Make the ultimate sacrifice to win.

♟ Against the wall

Can you find a two move sequence for White to checkmate Black?

CLUE: Corner the King.

♟ Sealed fate

Which White move leaves Black unable to prevent checkmate?

CLUE: Use the distant protection of a Bishop.

♟ Death threat

Can you see the two-move mate for White?

CLUE: Mate the black King in the corner.

For puzzle solutions see page 91.

The only way for a game of chess to be won or lost is if it ends in checkmate. A game that does not end in this way is called a *draw* – when neither player wins or loses. There are six different ways to draw in a game of chess:

No win situation

A game ends in *stalemate* if it is your turn to move, but there is no move that you can legally make. You cannot move your King without placing it in check, and if you also have Pawns they are locked and unable to move at all.)

White to move – but neither the King nor the Pawn can move. This is stalemate.

Perpetual check

Perpetual check happens when one player continually puts the other in check. It is often used by the losing player to escape checkmate and force a draw.

1. Kh1 Qf1+
2. Kh2 Qf2+
3. Kh1 Qf1+
4. Kh2 Qf2+

Wherever the white King goes, the black Queen follows – perpetual check.

Repetition of moves

If the same position occurs three times in one game, a player can claim a draw. This is similar to perpetual check – the game has reached a situation that is

Draw by agreement

If both players agree that they are equally matched in terms of material and position, and unlikely to reach a checkmate situation, they may agree to a draw.

Grandmaster Viswanathan Anand claims a victory – however, more tha half of all the chess games that are played at top levels end in a draw.

Nothing happening

When both players have made fifty moves without making a capture or a Pawn move, they may claim a draw. If they are still awake, that is. This is called the *fifty-move rule*.

Not enough firepower

Certain combinations of pieces in the endgame do not have the power to give checkmate. Th is called having *insufficient mating material*. I players realize this, they can agree to a draw without having to chase each other around th board to find out that neither can win! The following piece combinations are not enough to give checkmate:

You'll never take me...

● King and Bishop v. King
● King and Knight v. King
● King and two Knights v. King
● King v. King

Internet link
For a link to a Web site where you can find details and illustrated examples of each of the six different types of draw, go to
www.usborne-quicklinks.com

Chess tournaments

A chess competition is called a tournament. There are different types of tournament, but they all follow similar basic rules that are set out by official chess organizations.

♜ **Swiss system** As players win games, they play against progressively better players. (If they lose, they play against weaker players.) No-one is knocked out of this type of tournament.

♜ **Quads** Players are sorted into groups of similar ability. Each plays everyone else in the group to find a group winner. Gradually players are eliminated to leave one winner.

♜ **Correspondence** Players send their moves to each other written on a postcard. Games can last for years!

♜ **Internet** The Internet is a popular place to play chess for players of all levels, from beginners to Grandmasters.

Key words

draw A game that ends with no winner.

fifty-move rule If each player has made fifty consecutive moves without making a capture or a Pawn move, they may claim a draw.

insufficient mating material Too few pieces on the board for checkmate to be possible.

stalemate Happens when the player whose turn it is cannot move legally.

Internet link
For a link to a Web site where you can read about the 1993 Championship matches between Kasparov and Short, go to **www.usborne-quicklinks.com**

Garry Kasparov and Nigel Short took part in a fight for the title of World Champion in 1993. Chess at this level is exciting to watch and is often photographed or filmed for television.

KASPAROV   SHORT

THE TIMES WORLD CHESS CHAMPIONSHIP

Drawn game puzzles

Sometimes you will see that it is impossible for you to win a game of chess. In this kind of situation, the best thing to do is to force a draw. On these two pages are some puzzles that will help you spot the way to do this in different situations.

Did you know?

The shortest stalemate in theory in a game of chess would take only 12 moves – and no pieces would be exchanged.

Internet link
For a link to a Web site with more chess puzzles, go to www.usborne-quicklinks.com

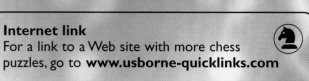

♟ Playing to draw

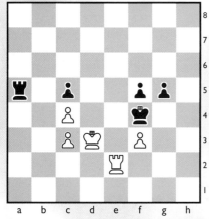

How can White force a stalemate to avoid eventual checkmate here?

CLUE: Sacrifice the Rook.

♟ Treacherous mate

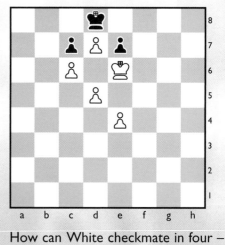

How can White checkmate in four – but avoid putting Black in stalemate?

CLUE: Move carefully to force responses from Black.

♟ Material loss

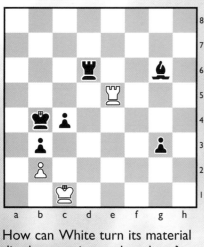

How can White turn its material disadvantage into a draw here?

CLUE: Use a check to force Black's move.

♚ Hidden King

Where would you place the black King so it is in stalemate?

CLUE: In which corner does White control the most squares?

For puzzle solutions see page 91.

♟ Bouncing King

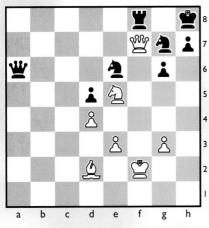

How can White use a sacrifice to good effect in forcing a draw here?

CLUE:
Go for perpetual check.

♟ Last-ditch attempt

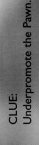

How should White move to prevent checkmate (and play for a draw)?

CLUE:
Underpromote the Pawn.

♟ Give it up

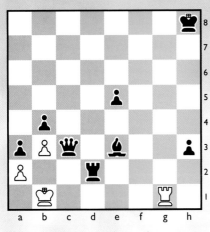

What can. White do to force a stalemate position on this board?

CLUE:
A swift sacrifice is the key.

♟ Missing royal

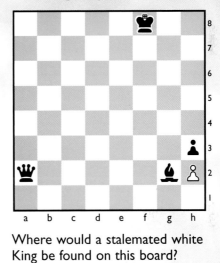

Where would a stalemated white King be found on this board?

CLUE:
It is in a place where its own Pawn restricts its movement.

♟ Futile promotion

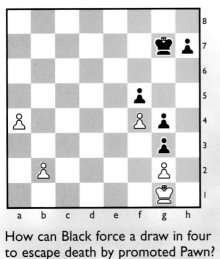

How can Black force a draw in four to escape death by promoted Pawn?

CLUE:
Black should use a Pawn to trap its own King.

♟ Fighting chance

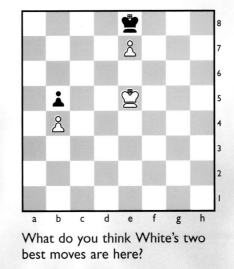

What do you think White's two best moves are here?

CLUE:
There is no need to play for stalemate – so don't!

For puzzle solutions see page 91.

The story of chess

The game of chess evolved from similar games over hundreds of years. People play different versions of chess all over the world. *Xiang Qi* (pronounced *shyang chi*), the Chinese version, is probably played by more people than any other game in the world.

Early games

Simple board games have been played for thousands of years, since the earliest civilizations. The game of chess appeared much later.

A fragment of a board game found at the site of Mohenjo-daro, an ancient city in Asia.

Shaturanga, the first truly chess-like game, is thought to have been invented in India, in the sixth century AD. It was a game for four players, designed to be played with a die on a chequered board with 64 squares, like a modern chess board.

In *Xiang Qi* (Chinese chess), the pieces are placed on points where lines cross, not on squares.

From Shaturanga to Shatranj

During the sixth century, changes were made to the rules of Shaturanga to accommodate Hindu law. Gambling was forbidden and so the use of dice was no longer allowed. The four armies merged to form two larger, opposing armies, in a game for two players. This new game was called Shatranj.

The birth of chess

There are different theories about how Shatranj evolved into the game of chess.

● Saracens (the Medieval name for Muslim Arabs) may have brought the game with them to Europe when they invaded Spain from North Africa.

● Charlemagne (King of the Holy Roman Empire in the ninth century, in what is now western and northern Europe) may have received a Shatranj set as a gift from a Byzantine empress. (The Byzantine Empire was in southern Europe, western Asia and northern Africa.)

● Knights may have brought the game back when they returned from the Crusades in the twelfth century.

This Isle of Lewis chess set was carved from walrus ivory. It dates from around the twelfth century and is one of the oldest-known chess set designs.

Key words

chess variant A game based on standard chess that has vital differences, for example different rules or a different board.

Internet link

For a link to a Web site where you can browse examples of the different chess variants from around the world, go to **www.usborne-quicklinks.com**

Setting the standard

The pieces that are used in international chess competitions are known as "Staunton" pieces. They were named after Howard Staunton, a famous chess player who approved their design in the 19th century. Staunton-type chess sets can be produced in almost any material but are usually wooden or plastic.

Staunton chess pieces have simple, stylized shapes.

A game for the world

From the Indian game of Shatranj, several distinct new games emerged all over the world, aside from chess:

● *Xiang Qi* **(Chinese chess)** This game uses points on its board instead of squares, and the opposing sides are separated by a central "river".

● *Shogi* **(Japanese chess)** A game in which pieces that have already been taken are allowed back on to the board.

● *Sittuyin* **(Burmese chess)** This version still makes use of the original horse and elephant pieces from Shatranj. In this game the players themselves decide how to arrange their pieces on the board at the start.

Variations on a theme

There are also many different games that are based on chess – these are collectively called chess variants:

● **Scotch game** The first player makes one move. The second player makes two moves. The first player goes again, with three moves, and so on. If either player gives check during their series of moves, their "turn" ends.

● **Fischerandom chess** In this variant, invented by Bobby Fischer, the back rank pieces are shuffled in random order, so that players cannot rely only on knowledge of opening lines to win a game.

● **Suicide chess** The objective in this variant is to be the first player to lose all your pieces!

● **Glinski's hexagonal chess** Invented in Poland, this is played mostly in eastern Europe, on a board made up of 91 hexagonal "cells".

● **Three-dimensional chess** Raumschach is the classic form of 3-D chess. It has also made appearances on Star Trek.

Mr. Spock thinks about his next move in a game of 3-D chess – he was beaten every time he played Captain Kirk on *Star Trek*.

The politics of chess

Chess might be "only a game", but some people take it very seriously indeed. It has been caught up in politics and riddled with cases of professional and personal rivalries and even long-standing feuds.

Governing chess

The *Fédération International des Echecs* (International Chess Federation), or FIDE* for short (pronounced *fee-day*) was set up in 1924 in Paris, to oversee chess playing internationally.

FIDE's motto is "we are one family". It aims to unite chess players worldwide.

Today, FIDE is still the main chess governing body, with 156 member federations from different countries, and over five million individual members worldwide. The president of FIDE is elected by its members. FIDE issues rules to tournaments and competitions, including the FIDE World Championship. It also awards titles like Grandmaster, International Master, Woman Grandmaster and others.

Chess rebels

● FIDE champion Bobby Fischer refused to play Anatoly Karpov, in 1975. FIDE made Karpov the new champion. However, Fischer and the US government claimed that the FIDE title was rightfully his.

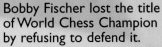

Bobby Fischer lost the title of World Chess Champion by refusing to defend it.

● Garry Kasparov broke away from FIDE to set up the Professional Chess Association in 1993. His first challenger was Nigel Short of the UK, but Kasparov held on to his title. He was beaten by Vladimir Kramnik in 2000. Kramnik now considers himself Champion.

Two champions

But who is the real World Champion? Since Kasparov left FIDE, there have been four FIDE World Champions:

1993–1999 Anatoly Karpov (Russia)
1999–2000 Alexander Khalifman (Russia)
2000–2001 Viswanathan Anand (India)
2001–   Ruslan Pomomariov (Ukraine) –
           at the age of only 18.

Moves are now being made to unify the World Championship title once more.

So what's the score?

Chess players are awarded an ELO rating according to their performance in tournament matches. Players with an ELO rating of 2000 or above may be awarded a FIDE rating. The ELO rating system is named after the Hungarian chess player Arpad Elo, who devised it as a way of accurately comparing the skills of players. FIDE adopted his system in 1970. Titles like Grandmaster and International Master are awarded by FIDE. To become a Grandmaster you need to earn three Grandmaster "norms" – performances rated above 2600 in a tournamnet where you play against three Grandmasters. You also need a FIDE rating of 2500 or above.

 *For the address of FIDE, see page 96.

A game for the masses

Chess became popular in the USSR (Soviet Union) after the Bolsheviks (communist workers) took power in the Russian Revolution in 1917. Lenin, the first Communist Party leader, was an avid chess player, describing the game as "the gymnasium of the mind". He was known for being gracious even in defeat.

Lenin supported the Bolsheviks' plan to encourage chess playing among the people of the USSR. Previously it had been a game played only by the rich and privileged members of society.

The Bolsheviks hoped that playing chess would encourage rational, logical thoughts among the Soviet people that would help them to follow the ideals of communism.

Illegal yogurt

In a tense match between fellow Russians Viktor Korchnoi and Anatoly Karpov in 1978, Korchnoi's team accused Karpov's team of cheating. How? By allegedly supplying Karpov with coded messages in the form of yogurt.

The chess authorities took quick action, and Karpov was, from that point in the tournament on, allowed only one particular variety of yogurt, served at a specified time by a waiter. He went on to win the match anyway.

Listen very carefully...

Legacy of champions

The USSR joined FIDE for the first time in 1946. Soon after, Mikhail Botvinnik became the first in a long line of Soviet champions. He went on to found a chess school that would later be attended by Karpov, Kasparov and Kramnik.

Since 1948, chess players from Russia and other former Soviet republic states have completely dominated the World Championships. (Between 1948 and 1972 no non-Soviet player claimed the title.)

Since the break up of the Soviet Union in 1991, less money has been spent on chess training for young players by Russia and the former Soviet republics. However, the legacy of generations of great chess players remains, and players from this region continue to dominate the chess world even today.

This is a swimming pool in Hungary, where a group of men are playing chess. Chess is popular in many eastern European countries.

Internet link
For a link to a Web site where you can read all the latest FIDE news and information, go to
www.usborne-quicklinks.com

Chess celebrities

The players on the next four pages have all been World Champion. The dates in brackets show when they held their titles.

Internet link
For a link to a Web site with links to biographical information about Chess Champions from Steinitz to Kasparov, go to **www.usborne-quicklinks.com**

Wilhelm Steinitz (1886–1894)

Wilhelm Steinitz of Bohemia (now the Czech Republic) was the first professional chess player, playing chess to earn money while he was a student in Vienna, in Austria. However, he never made enough to retire, and played chess until he had a mental breakdown. He developed the idea that a series of small advantages eventually add up to a large positional advantage in a game situation. This revolutionized the way people thought about chess at the time.

Emanuel Lasker (1894–1921)

The German Emanuel Lasker became World Champion at the age of 25. At first, people doubted his victory over the much older defending champion, Steinitz. He silenced his critics by beating Steinitz when they next played.

Lasker demanded large fees for appearances. After retiring from chess, he played bridge professionally. At the age of 65, he was forced to leave Nazi Germany for America, and had to return to playing chess for money.

José Raúl Capablanca (1921–1927)

José Raúl Capablanca was born in Cuba and learned chess at the age of four. At twelve years old, he beat the Cuban chess champion. He went to university in America and beat the US champion at the age of 20.

In 1921, Lasker resigned his title to Capablanca, who became known for his apparently effortless style of play. After Capablanca's death, Alekhine, his great rival, conceded that the world had lost "a very great chess genius".

Alexander Alekhine (1927–1935, 1937–1946)

At the time when Alexander Alekhine (born in the Soviet Union) challenged Capablanca for the title of World Champion, there were more world-class chess players around than ever before.

He took the title from Capablanca, but later lost it to Max Euwe, possibly as a result of poor preparation or alcoholism. In a rematch, he managed to beat Euwe, regaining his title.

Max Euwe (1935–1937)

Max Euwe, from the Netherlands, was an amateur chess player. In his day job, he was a professor of mathematics and mechanics. He succeeded in beating Alekhine to win the champion's title (which Alekhine later won back from him).

When he retired from his academic profession, he became the president of FIDE* (*Fédération Internationale des Echecs*), between 1970 and 1978.

Mikhail Botvinnik (1948–1957, 1958–1960, 1961–1963)

Following the death of Alekhine, a tournament was organized to find the new World Champion, which Mikhail Botvinnik won – the first Russian to hold the title. Botvinnik set up a training programme for Russian chess players**. Training included physical exercise, playing against strong players, studying analyses of games and playing under difficult conditions.

Vasily Smyslov (1957–1958)

The Russian Vasily Smyslov held the title of World Champion for only a year. As well as chess, he loved music, and during the interval in his match against Botvinnik for the champion's title, he sang opera to the audience. He had almost become an opera singer with the Bolshoi, but had decided to take up chess as his career after narrowly failing the audition. He continued to play chess competitively until an old age – he was still playing in his seventies.

Mikhail Tal (1960–1961)

Latvian Mikhail Tal didn't play chess seriously until he was a teenager, but once he did take it up he found it hard to stop. Even when in hospital after an operation, he managed to slip out several times to a nearby chess club.

When he became World Champion he was only 24, making him the youngest champion up until then. He was famous for the complicated combinations he used to obliterate the opposition.

Tigran Petrosian (1963–1969)

Tigran Petrosian was born in Georgia, to Armenian parents. His style of chess was influenced by the hypermodern*** theories of Aron Nimzowitsch, and he liked to play closed games that challenged other Grandmasters very effectively but were difficult for non-masters to understand. For this reason, he was not a particularly popular World Champion, although he held the title for six years.

*For more about FIDE, see page 78.
**For more about the Russians and chess, see page 79.
***For more about hypermodernism, see page 34.

Boris Spassky (1969–1972)

The Russian Boris Spassky was admired as a World Champion not only for his chess playing abilities, but also for being polite and friendly!

The American Bobby Fischer challenged him for the title in 1972. This was during the Cold War between East and West, so both players were under pressure from their countries to win. The Russians suspected that Fischer's chair had been tampered with to make it affect Spassky's play – but never proved anything.

Robert Fischer (1972–1975)

American Bobby Fischer started playing chess when he was six, and at fifteen became the youngest ever Grandmaster up until then. He was Champion for three years, but lost the title when he refused to play the challenger, Anatoly Karpov, in 1975. Since then, Bobby Fischer has not played in public. People sometimes report playing him on the Internet but it is difficult to prove this. He is still highly-rated and some people consider him to be the best chess player of all time. It is said that he can remember every detail and move of every game he has ever played.

Anatoly Karpov (1975–1985, FIDE 1993–1999)

Although the Russian Anatoly Karpov gained the title of World Champion by default, after Bobby Fischer refused to play for it, he quickly proved that he deserved the title by winning many subsequent chess tournaments.

He was beaten in 1985 by Garry Kasparov, after the longest tournament match in chess history (six months). However, he later regained the FIDE* title of World Champion when Kasparov split with FIDE to form his own Professional Chess Association in 1993.

Garry Kasparov (FIDE 1985–1993, PCA 1993–1998, unofficial 1998–2000)

Russian Garry Kasparov attended the Botvinnik Chess School, and became a Grandmaster on his seventeenth birthday. He was FIDE Champion for eight years, after beating Anatoly Karpov, at the age of 22.

In 1993, Kasparov set up the PCA*. He was PCA World Champion until it disbanded in 1998, and then continued to call himself World Champion until Vladimir Kramnik beat him in 2000.

*For more about FIDE and the PCA, see page 78.

Alexander Khalifman (FIDE 1999–2000)

Alexander Khalifman was born in 1966 in Leningrad (now called St. Petersburg) in Russia, and started playing chess at the age of six. He became a Grandmaster in 1990 at the age of 24. He held the title of World Champion for a year, winning the championship even though he was nowhere near being the world's highest-rated* player at the time. He now plays professional chess in Germany and runs a chess academy in St. Petersburg.

Viswanathan Anand (FIDE 2000–2001)

Viswanathan Anand was born in 1969 in India. He learned to play chess at the age of six, and became Indian National Champion at the age of 16. His highest rating is number two in the world (PCA and FIDE). Viswanathan Anand seems to collect nicknames, among them: "Vishy, the Tiger of Madras" and "The One-Man Indian Chess Revolution".

Vladimir Kramnik (unoffical 2000–present)

Vladimir Kramnik was born in 1975 in Russia, and by the time he was five was already attending professional chess clubs. He went to the Botvinnik Chess School, like Kasparov and Karpov before him. He claims that the secret to beating Kasparov lies in not being scared of playing him, and is famous for his calmness whilst under pressure.

Ruslan Ponomariov (FIDE 2001–2002)

The Ukrainian Ruslan Ponomariov was born in 1983. At 14, he became the youngest Grandmaster in the world at that time, and in January 2002, he became FIDE World Chess Champion at the age of only 18, making him the youngest person ever to claim the title of World Champion.

Future electronic champions?

Computer programmers know their software cannot often beat the very best human chess players. Even though computers don't have "off days", their powers of analysis, however fast, are still only as good as the brains that designed them. One of the latest chess "supercomputers" is called *Deep Fritz*. World champion Vladimir Kramnik faced *Deep Fritz for a showdown in 2002, and the match ended in a draw.*

Internet link
For a link to a Web site where you can read a fascinating article about the 1972 Fischer-Spassky World Championship game, go to **www.usborne-quicklinks.com**

*For more about the ratings system, see page 78.

Champions of the future

Until recently, chess has been a very male-dominated sport. Lots of rising stars are now women. Computers also keep improving, and may one day rule the chess world.

Judit Polgar

Judit Polgar, born in 1976 in Hungary, is the world's highest-ranked woman chess player ever. She became the only woman ever to have beaten Garry Kasparov in a chess match in 2002. She has never taken the title of women's World Chess Champion, preferring to set her sights on the men's World Championship title.

Judit Polgar has two sisters who are also successful competitive chess players. One runs a chess academy in New York. Their parents encouraged all three sisters to excel at chess from a young age, preferring the sport over mathematics.

At 15, Judit Polgar became the youngest player ever to be awarded the title of Grandmaster, beating Bobby Fischer's previous record. (Her record was subsequently broken by Ruslan Ponomariov, when he was 14.)

Judit Polgar is renowned for her fierce, attacking style of chess playing.

Zhu Chen

The 2001–2002 women's World Chess Champion was Zhu Chen of China. Born in 1976, she started to play Chinese chess when she was five and learned chess at age seven. She is currently at university in China, and is married to a chess Grandmaster from Qatar.

Zhu Chen becomes women's World Chess Champion in Moscow, 2002.

Alexandra Kosteniuk

The Russian player Alexandra Kosteniuk became 2001–2002 women's World Chess Vice-Champion at the age of 17, after being beaten by Zhu Chen in the final. She had already achieved the title Woman Grandmaster at the age of 14, and had also already achieved the title of International Master among men.

She was born in Russia in 1984, and was taught by her father to play chess. To help her succeed, he made her memorize the names and colours of all the squares on a chess board, and tested her until she knew the chess board inside-out.

Alexandra Kosteniuk, dressed to promote chess.

Internet link
For a link to a Web site where you can find out all about Judit Polgar with links to biographical information, interviews, articles, games and photographs, go to
www.usborne-quicklinks.com

The first chess machine

The first chess-playing machine was designed by American Wolfgang von Kempelen in 1770. It looked like a man dressed in oriental costume, sat at a chess board. The machine was nicknamed "the Turk". People believed that the machine could play chess by itself, even though now we know that it must have been operated by a human.

This picture shows a chess-playing automaton similar to the Turk. The mechanical workings may have concealed a human operator.

Champion chips

Modern chess computers actually do have the ability to evaluate billions of different positions themselves and "decide" on the best move to make. It is this calculating ability that may one day give chess computers the potential to beat even the very best humans all the time.

Deep Blue was the fastest chess computer in the world when it beat Kasparov in 1997. (The faster the computer, the more calculations it makes, and the more positions it compares.) *Deep Blue* didn't even have to calculate every single position – it could discount irrelevant searches to save time.

The chip from *Deep Blue's* processor. It is small enough to fit in the palm of your hand.

How a chess computer works

All chess computer programs work in a similar way. Their software has an "evaluation function" that uses mathematical formulas to compare possible board positions.

For example, *Deep Blue's* software allowed it to evaluate four factors: material, position, King safety and tempo. Each possible position was then given a score. A positive score meant a good position for White; a negative score was a good position for Black.

A screenshot from a home computer program called Chessmaster.

Mind-blowing possibilities

At the start of a game, White has 20 possible moves. Black has 20 possible responses to each of White's possible moves, making a total of 400 possibilities, just for the first two moves. By the end of White's second move, there are 8,000 different possible positions.

Within ten moves, there are an incredible 10 trillion positions for the computer to evaluate. This is why chess-playing computers need extremely powerful processors.

Internet link
For a link to a Web site where you can find out all about how chess computers make their calculations, go to **www.usborne-quicklinks.com**

Chess words

algebraic notation The standard method of recording chess games. It uses letters and numbers to identify squares on the board, and letter codes for the pieces. An example of algebraic notation would read as follows:
1. e4 e5
2. Nf3 Nf6.
This describes a typical sequence of two opening moves – each player advances a Pawn to the centre of the board, then develops a Knight to support the Pawn.

anchorage Support provided from behind by Pawns for pieces that may be unable to escape from long-range attacks quickly, like Knights.

back rank mate A type of checkmate where the King is trapped on the back rank by its own pieces (often the same pieces that were intended to defend it) and is unable to move away from an attack.

backward Pawn A Pawn that has been left behind by the adjacent Pawns. It is vulnerable to attack as it cannot rely on the support of other Pawns.

bad Bishop A Bishop that its trapped behind its own pieces. An example of this would be a black-squared Bishop surrounded by Pawns that occupy black squares.

castling A special move for a King and Rook. The King moves two spaces towards the Rook, and the Rook jumps over the King to the space next to it. This protects the King and brings the Rook nearer to the middle of its rank where it can effectively attack open files.

check An attack on the King.

checkmate An attack on the King which cannot be defended. This is the end of the game and the checkmated player loses.

checking piece A piece that attacks the King.

chess clock A special clock with two faces that records the time each player spends on moves in a chess game. If a player runs out of time in a tournament game, they lose.

chess variant A game based on standard chess that has vital differences, for example different rules or a different board. Some famous examples of chess variants include Suicide Chess, Fischerandom Chess, Scotch Chess, Hexagonal Chess and 3-D Chess.

closed diagonal A diagonal that is blocked by pieces.

closed game A strategy that keeps the attacking pieces behind a strong Pawn structure until the game is in progress. This results in a board that is crowded with pieces and sometimes the position can become blocked, where neither player is able to make effective attacks or advances.

counter-attack A way of responding to an attack by posing a new attack.

dangerous/non-dangerous corner The corner square on which a King is exposed to/safe from the opposing Bishop.

development Moving pieces from their starting positions during the opening stage to positions where they will be useful in the next stage of the game.

diagonal A line of diagonal squares.

discovered attack A piece moves to reveal an attack from a different piece.

discovered check A piece moves to reveal an attack on the enemy King from a different piece.

double check A piece moves to give check, revealing another checking piece at the same time. The result is two different checks on the King at once.

doubled Rooks Two Rooks of the same colour on next-door squares. These form an extremely powerful attacking force – if one attacks and is taken, the other Rook can immediately attack the same square.

double Pawns Two Pawns of the same colour on the same file. This is a weak position for two Pawns as they cannot defend each other and block each other's movements.

draw A game that ends with no winner.

en passant The rule that allows a Pawn to capture another that has moved forwards two squares, and in doing so, bypassed the threat of capture. The attacking Pawn moves to the square it would have captured the other Pawn on had it only moved one square.

exchange Trading a piece for an opposing piece of the same type or that has the same value.

exchange advantage The player with pieces of greater combined value following an exchange has the advantage.

fair exchange Pieces of a similar value are exchanged and neither side loses out.

fianchetto An opening move that places a Bishop on the longest diagonal where it can threaten many squares. The Bishop moves to the square that was originally occupied by either the b-Pawn or the g-Pawn.

fifty-move rule If either player has made fifty consecutive moves without there being a capture or a Pawn move, they may claim a draw.

file A line of squares that runs from the top to the bottom of the board.

flank One of the edges of the board.

fork A sneaky move – a piece moves to a square from where it can threaten two or more opposing pieces at once. Only one piece can escape the attack – the other will be captured on the next turn.

gambit A move made during the opening stage of the game, that offers a Pawn or a minor piece to the opponent, in return for better positions for the pieces on the board.

good Bishop – a Bishop that is not trapped by its own pieces. For example, a black-squared Bishop that is surrounded by its own Pawns that occupy black squares will be unable to move freely.

hypermodern A movement in chess that started in the 1920s, where a player ignores the most usual method of developing pieces and Pawns to the central squares early on in the game. Instead, the hypermodern player aims to control the centre using pieces placed at a distance.

initiative Had by the player who is directing the course of the game.

insufficient mating material Too few pieces on the board for checkmate to be possible.

Kingside The four files on the two Kings' side of the board.

losing a tempo Losing time – usually a bad thing, especially in the opening stage of the game, when the race is on to develop your pieces. However, you may choose to lose a tempo, for example if you are trying to gain the opposition when advancing your King during the endgame.

material The pieces that are left on the board.

material advantage/disadvantage Having pieces of a greater/lesser combined value than the enemy's.

mating net Pieces placed in such a way that wherever the enemy King moves, it will be trapped.

mobility The ability of pieces to move freely.

open file A file that is not blocked by Pawns.

open game A strategy that develops the pieces quickly, positioning them in front of the Pawns. This type of game often leads to lots of attacks and exchanges early on, opening up lines on the board.

opening The stage between the first moves of the game and the completion of piece development.

open lines Ranks, files or diagonals that are clear of pieces.

opposition When a square separates two advancing Kings, the player that moved last is said to have the opposition. The opposing King cannot move nearer or it would be in check, and so must move aside or move away.

outpost A square that cannot be attacked by opposing Pawns.

overloaded piece A piece that has more than one defensive job to do, leaving the pieces it is defending open to attack.

overprotection Defence of a square by more than one piece.

passed Pawn A Pawn that has left the opposing Pawns on adjacent files behind, and so has a good chance of promoting (as it is less likely to be captured).

Pawn chain Two or more Pawns on adjacent files arranged along a diagonal. Each Pawn is protected by the one behind. The enemy can only safely attack the base of the chain.

Pawn island A group of Pawns cut off from the others. They are vulnerable to attack.

Pawn structure The way your Pawns are arranged.

perpetual check A player is put in check repeatedly but cannot be checkmated. The result is a draw. Typically the checked King will jump between two squares, as it is checked, escapes, and is checked again.

pin An attack on a piece that is shielding one of greater value.

pinned piece A piece that must stay still to protect another piece of greater value.

plan A series of moves designed to achieve a particular aim, for example to promote a Pawn, castle the King or checkmate the opponent. It is important to have a plan for every stage of the game you are at

position A measure of the amount of attacking control that you have over the squares on the board.

promotion When a Pawn reaches the other end of the board and can be swapped for a more powerful piece, usually a Queen.

queening square The square on the far side of the board that a Pawn needs to reach to gain promotion (usually to a Queen, but it may be any other piece).

Queenside The four files on the Queens' side of the board.

rank A line of squares that runs from the left to the right of the board.

sacrifice The deliberate loss of a piece as part of a strategy.

skewer An attack that forces a valuable piece to move, exposing one of less value to attack.

smothered mate The King is completely surrounded by its own pieces and so cannot move out of checkmate.

stalemate The player whose turn it is cannot move legally, but is not in checkmate. The result is a draw.

tempo (pl. tempi) A unit of time in chess – equivalent to a single move.

triple Pawns Three Pawns of the same colour on the same file. They are vulnerable as they cannot protect each other and block each other's movement.

variation In an opening strategy, a variation is a unique combination of moves that develop from a particular type of opening.

zugzwang This is a German word that means "forced to move". If a player must make a move that leads to a worse position or even checkmate, they are in a *zugzwang* position.

Puzzle solutions

King puzzles 15

King puzzle 1 1. Kd5 (White forks two Knights).

King puzzle 2 1. Ke2++.

King puzzle 3 1... Kc7++.

King puzzle 4 1. Kf4 g3, 2. hxg2++.

Knight puzzles 23

Knight puzzle 1. Nxg4 (Knight also now forks black King and Rook).

Piece puzzles 30–31

Pawn puzzle 1 1. gxh3 is the best white move – otherwise Black will promote its Pawn.

Pawn puzzle 2 The g-Pawn – 1. h6 gxh6, 2. g7 (Black cannot now stop the Pawn promoting), 3. g8 (Q).

Knight puzzle 1. Nb6+ Qxb6, 2. cxb6.

Bishop puzzle 1 1. Bh3+ or 1. Bd3+. Bh3+ is better as it skewers the Black Queen, instead of the Rook. White can then take the Queen on its next turn.

Bishop puzzle 2 1. Bb2++.

Rook puzzle 1... Rb4+. Black forks the White King and Knight, so will be able to take the Knight next turn after the King has moved out of check.

Queen puzzle 1 Five ways to check with the Queen: 1. Qf2+ wins Rook on g1; 2. Qd4+ wins Rook on a7; 1. Qd6+ wins Knight on b8; 1. Qc3+ wins Bishop on c8; 1. Qb2+ wins Pawn on b5.

Queen puzzle 2 1... Qb8++. White's a-Pawn cannot capture the Queen as it is pinned to the King by the Black Rook on a1.

King puzzle 1 1... Kc7++.

King puzzle 2 1. 0-0++. An example of late castling.

The Indian problem (in Did you know? box) 1. Kb1 b4, 2. Bc1 b5, 3. Rd2 Kf4, 4. Rd4++.

Middlegame puzzles 48–49

The right move 1. Bd8++.

Nowhere to run 1. Ne6++.

Well-placed piece 1. Bxf6++. The white Bishop moves to reveal a double check on the Black King from which it cannot escape.

Two-move mate 1. Rh5+ gxh5, 2. Qxh5++.

Defending the King 1 1. Re5++.

Defending the King 2 1. Bf4++ or 1. Ba5++. The white Bishop moves to reveal a further discovered check from one of its Rooks.

Defending the King 3 1. Rd6++. The Rook cannot be taken by either of the Pawns as they are pinned to the King by White's Bishop and Queen.

Square overload White can make use of a barrage of attacks on the same square to crush Black's defence here – 1. Qh8+ Rxh8, 2. Rh8++.

Noble sacrifice 1. Qxh7+, Kxh7, 2. Rh5++. The Black King cannot escape – the squares are cut off by White's Knight on e7.

Deadly initiative 1... Bd3++. The White King is caught in a web of attacks from the black Bishop, Rook and Queen and Pawn.

Tactical tricks puzzles 52–53

Slice the defence 1. e5+ Kxe5, 2. Bg7+ Kd5/Kf5 (Black King has to move, leaving skewered Rook exposed), 3. Bxa1.

Don't get pinned down 1... Qxb4+, 2. Kxb4, Ra4+. Black has skewered the White Queen.

Lethal weapon 1... Ne3, 2. fxe3 (White must take the Knight to avoid immediately losing its Queen) Qh4+, 3. g3 Qxg3++.

Cutlery crusade 1. Bc5+ Qxc5 (White's Bishop forks the Black Queen and Knight, but is captured), 2. Ne6+ (White forks again, forcing the King to move), 3. Nxc5 (the white Knight takes the Black Queen).

Protected Pawn 1... Be6+, 2. Kxe6. The White King shields Black's Pawn from White's Rook.

Rook revenge 1. Rh8 Rxa7, 2. Rh7+. White skewers the black King to win the Rook.

Battle of the Bishops 1. Qxc6 Bxc6, 2. Bxc6++. A Bishop pin followed by a Queen sacrifice.

Forked lightning 1. Rf8+ Ke5, 2. Nc6+. A Knight fork means that White will capture Black's Rook next.

Widen the gap 1. Be8+ Kxe8, 2. Nd6+. Once Black loses the Queen it cannot hope to win this game.

Inevitable capture 1. Qd5+. Queen fork by White.

Combination puzzles 56–57

Checkmate surprise 1. Ng1 Bc7, 2. Nf3++ **or** 1. Ng1 g4, 2. g3++.

Push for victory 1. Qxf7+ Rxf7, 2. Re8++.

Weak spot 1. Qxh5+ Rxh5, 2. Bg6++.

Wrongfooted Rooks 1. Qxh6 Bxh6, 2. Rxh6++.

Tragedy for the King 1. Qxd7+ Kd7, 2. Bf5+ Ke8,

3. Bd7+ Kf8, 4. Bxe7++ **or** 1. Qxd7+ Kd7, 2. Bf5+ Kc6, 3. Bd7++.

Spoilt for choice 1. Qf4+ Kxc5, 2. Qd4++ **or** 1. Qf4+ Kd5, 2. Qd4++.

Early mate 1. Qh6 Bxh6, 2. Ne7++ **or** 1. Qh6 Bxf6, 2. Nxf6+ Kh8, 3. Qxh7++ **or** 1.Qh6 Bxf6, 2. Nxf6+ Qxf6, 3. exf6 (whatever Black does now, White's next move is inevitable), 4. Qg7++.

Inevitable defeat 1... Bg1+, 2. Kxg1 Qxe1+, 3. Qf1 Qxf1+, 4. Kh2 Qh1++ **or** 1... Bg1+, 2. Rgxg1 Nf1+ (double check), 3. Kg2/Kh1 Qh2++ **or** 1... Bg1+, 2. Rexg1 Nf1+ (double check), 3. Kh1 Rxh3+, 4. Rh2 Rxh2++.

Humble mate 1. Qe1 Rxe1 (releasing White Pawn from pin), 2. g2++.

Long-term goal 1. Rg4+ fxg4, 2. Qg5+ Kh8, 3. Qh6, Qd8/Raa8, 4. Qxh7++ **or** 1. Rg4+ fxg4, 2. Qg5+ Kh8, 3. Qh6 f5/Bxd3, 4. Qxf8++.

Sacrifice puzzles 60–61

Bury the King 1. Qg7+ Nxg7, 2. Nf6++.

Sacrificial barrage 1... Qxb2+, 2. Kxb2 Rgb8++.

Building a wall 1. Rd8+ Rxd8 (White's Queen is now released from the pin), 2. Qxa7++.

King-baiting 1... Bb4+, 2. Kxb4 Qa5++.

Coming from behind 1. Nb6+ axb6, 2. Ra4++.

Brave monarch 1. Qg8+ Rxg8 (White sacrifices its Queen in order to trap the Black King in a web of its own pieces), 2. Nf7++.

Danger all around 1. Qxg6+ hxg6, 2. Rh8++.

Piledriver 1. Qxa7+ Kxa7 (White sacrifices the Queen as part of a mating combination), Ra2+ Qa4, 3. Rxa4++.

Wriggling free 1... Qg3+, 2. Kxg3 e1(Q)+, 3. Kh3 Re3+, 4.Kh2 Qg3++ **or** 1... Qg3+, 2. Kxg3 e1(Q)+, 3. Kh2 Qxh4+, 4. Kg1 Re1++.

Closing in 1. Qxf7+ Bxf7, 2. Rxc8+ Be8, 3. Rxe8++.

Endgame puzzles 64–65

Mate surprise 1. Be5 Qe8 (Black defends against a White underpromotion) 2. f8(N)++ , 2. Bf5++.

Sticky end 1. Rc2 Bd2, 2. Raxb2++ **or** 1. Rc2 Kxc2/Kxa2, 2. Na3++ **or** 1. Rc2 Kxa2/Nxc2/bxc2, 2. Nc3++/Na3++.

Cavalry charge 1. Ba4 d6, 2. Nbc7++ **or** 1. Ba4 e4, 2. Qxe4++ **or** 1. Ba4 f6, 2. Ndc7++ **or** 1. Ba4 f5, 2. Qg8++.

King pressure 1. Kg8 Qxg5+, 2. Bg7++ **or** 1. Kg8 Rxf6+, 2. Qxf6++ **or** 1. Kg8 Qb1, 2. Nf7++.

Forced to move 1. Qd1 Kd3, 2. Rxd5++ **or** 1. Qd1

Kc5, 2. Qg1++ **or** 1. Qd1, Kxe5, 2. d4++.

Defensive collapse 1. Qxg7+ Rxg7, 2. Rxg7++.

Impending doom 1. Qxd4++.

Best move 1. Nd7+. This move puts the Black King in check, forcing it to move, so the Queen cannot take White's passed Pawn on f7. At the same time, the black Knight protects the Pawn's queening square (f8) so the Pawn can safely promote on White's next turn.

Good clean fun 1. Kg6 Kg8, 2. Rc8++ **or** 1. Kf7 Kg8, 2. Rc8++.

Cornered King 1. Qxf6 gxf6, 2. Rg1+ Kh8, 3. Bxf6++.

Checkmate puzzles 70–71

Walled-in King 1. Qh6++.

Discovered doom 1. Be7++.

Surrounded! 1. Qh8++.

Humble attacker 1. Rb7++.

Repeated blows 1. Rf7+ Kg8, 2. Rxe8++.

Buried alive 1. Qg7+ Nxg7, 2. Nh6++.

Sealed fate 1. Rh6+ gxh6, 2. Qg8++.

King in the bag 1. Qd6+ Kf6, 2. e5++.

Against the wall 1. Qg6+ Kh8, 2. Rf8++.

Double death threat 1. Ra8+ Kxa8, 2. Qa7++.

Drawn game puzzles 74–75

Playing to draw 1. Ra2 Rxa2. Stalemate.

Material loss 1. Rb5+ Kxb5. Stalemate.

Treacherous mate 1. Ke5 e6, 2. d6 cxd6, 3. Kxd6 e5, 4. c7++.

Hidden King The King should be placed on the h1 square to be in a stalemate position.

Bouncing King 1. Qxf8+ Nxf8, 2. Nf7+ Kg8, 3. Nh6+ Kh8. The Black King is in perpetual check – stalemate.

Give it up 1. Rg8+ Kxg8. Stalemate.

Futile promotion 1... Kg6/Kh6, 2. a5 Kh5, 3. a6 Kh4, 4. a7 h5, 5. a8 (Q). Black has no legal moves left, so it is stalemate.

Last-ditch attempt 1. e8(N) – by underpromoting, White manages to stay in the game long enough to play for a draw.

Missing royal The King should be placed on the g1 square to be in a stalemate position.

Fighting chance 1. Kd6 is the best move for White to play for a win. The Black King will have to move aside, allowing the White Pawn to promote – white then stands a chance of winning the game. (1. Ke6 would force stalemate and this would be a draw – better for Black.)

Index

A

Alekhine, Alexander 62, 80, 81
algebraic notation 10, 11, 86
Anand, Viswanathan (Vishy) 72, 83
anchorage 23, 26, 86
attacking 26, 27, 32, 33, 36, 37, 40, 44,
   46, 58, 59, 62
   in the middlegame 48
   pieces 16, 20, 23, 27, 35, 58, 62, 63, 87
   squares 54
   the King 66–67
   with Bishops 20
   with Knights 23
   with Pawns 24–25
   with Rooks 19
   with the King 12, 14
   using tactical tricks 50, 51

B

back rank, the 9, 14, 40, 55, 63, 68, 69, 77
   mate 14, 15, 63, 86
Bishops 20–21, 29, 37, 69, 72
   bad, 21, 27, 62, 86
   fianchettoed, 43, 87
   good, 21, 62, 87
   moves 11
   puzzles 30
   value 28
board
   diagrams 10, 11
   edges 22, 23, 68, 69
   positions 45, 48, 85
   set-up 9
Bolsheviks 79
Botvinnik, Mikhail 79, 81
   chess school 79, 82, 83
Burmese chess, see *Sittuyin*

C

Caissa (patron goddess of chess) 70
Capablanca, José Raúl 80
Caro-Kann, the (opening) 34, 40
Carroll, Lewis 35
castling 12, 13, 15, 18, 33, 34, 36, 55, 56, 86
   Kingside 13, 34, 26, 42
   notation 10
   Queenside 13, 42

centre of the board 20, 22, 24, 25, 26, 29,
   33, 34, 40, 42, 62
Charlemagne 76
check 12, 13, 14, 19, 29, 37, 51, 56, 66–67, 72, 86, 88
   announcing, 52
   notation 10
checking pieces 12, 13, 66, 67, 86, 87
checkmate 12, 13, 14, 18, 19, 21, 29, 37, 43, 52, 54,
   56, 60, 64, 66, 67, 68–69, 70, 72, 73, 86
   early, 48, 62
   in four (see also Scholar's Mate) 59
   notation, 10
   puzzles 70–71
   quickest, 47
chess
   books 37
   clocks 45, 86
   clubs 54
   computers 32, 83, 85
   history of, 76–77
   in films and novels 35
   matches 32
   on the Internet 6–7, 73, 82
   organizations 73, 78
   pieces 23, 24, 30, 35
   politics 78–79
   theory 34, 35, 37
   variants 76, 87
Chess Player's Chronicle, The 31
Chinese chess, see *Xiang Qi*
closed games 35, 41, 46, 81, 87
Cold War, the 82
combinations (of moves) 34, 41, 56
combined force (of pieces) 68, 72
Communist Party, the 79
controlling
   centre of the board, the 33, 34, 35, 37, 38, 39
   game, the 41
   diagonals 21
   space 46, 55
   squares 19, 20, 32, 37, 55
corners 20, 69, 87
counter-attacking 37, 43, 87
Crusades, the 76

D

damage limitation 58, 59
Dame, die 16
dame, la 16
Deep Blue 32, 85
Deep Fritz 83
defending 27, 37, 44, 59
   against pins and skewers 50
   more than one piece 47
   space 46
   with Pawns 24, 25, 26, 55

Acknowledgements

Every effort has been made to trace the copyright holders of the material in this book.
If any rights have been omitted, the publishers offer to rectify this in any future edition,
following notification. The publishers are grateful to the following organizations and
individuals for their contribution and permission to reproduce material.

Photography credits (t = top, m = middle, b = bottom, l = left, r = right)

Cover ©Michael Neveux/CORBIS;
p1 ©George B. Diebold/corbisstockmarket.com;
p2 ©Wartenberg/Picture Press/CORBIS;
p4 ©Lawrence Lawley/PhotoDisc;
p8 (bl) ©Hulton-Deutsch Collection/CORBIS;
p13 (tl) ©Burstein Collection/CORBIS; (m) ©Archivo Iconografico, S.A./CORBIS;
p23 (r) ©Archivo Iconografico S.A./CORBIS;
p26 (bl) ©Dover Publications;
p29 (br) ©Hulton-Deutsch Collection/CORBIS;
p32 (br) ©Najlah Feanny/CORBIS SABA;
p34 (br) courtesy of the Edward Winter Collection;
p35 (r) courtesy of Warner Bros.
HARRY POTTER, characters, names and related indicia are trademarks of and © Warner Bros.
(s02)
Harry Potter Publishing Rights © J.K. Rowling;
p37 (l) courtesy of the State Library of Victoria, Melbourne, Victoria, Australia;
p41 (tr) ©Bettmann/CORBIS;
p44 (br) courtesy of the Edward Winter Collection; **p45** (tr) Image 100/Royalty-Free/CORBIS;
p50 (tr) courtesy of the Edward Winter Collection;
p62 (tr) courtesy of the Edward Winter Collection;
p66 (l), **p67** (bl) ©Walter Hodges/CORBIS;
p72 (tr) ©Despotovic Dusko/CORBIS SYGMA; **p73** (b) ©Touhig Sion/CORBIS SYGMA;
p76 (tl) ©CORBIS; (bl) ©Richard Bickel/CORBIS; (br) ©The British Museum; **p77** (br) ©Bettmann/CORBIS;
p78 (tl) courtesy of FIDE; (tr) ©Bettmann/CORBIS; **p79** ©Barry Lewis/CORBIS;
p80 (l) all courtesy of the Edward Winter Collection; **p81** (l) all courtesy of the Edward Winter Collection;
p82 (tl) ©Bettmann/CORBIS; (l) courtesy of the Edward Winter Collection;
(l) ©Hulton-Deutsch Collection/CORBIS; (bl) ©Richard Schulman/CORBIS;
p83 (tl) courtesy of the Chesspawn Web site; (l) ©Despotovic Dusko/CORBIS;
(l) ©Ruet Stephane/CORBIS; (bl) permission granted by Chess-Sector Web site;
p84 (bl) Copes Van Hasselt Johan/CORBIS SYGMA; (tr) ©Photo ITAR-TASS;
(br) courtesy of courtesy of the Kosteniuk Web site;
p85 (tl) Laurence Kesterson/CORBIS SYGMA; (bl) courtesy of Chessmaster;
(br) Bettmann/CORBIS;
p86–89 (b) ©Malcolm Piers/Image Bank.

All additional photography by Adam Constantine.

Chess pieces and boards for in-house photography provided by The London Chess Centre.